THE ROOF OF AF[

Narrated by Derek Groves

Commentary by Jon Amos

Foreword by Chris Bonington

Alfresco Books

First published in 1999 by *Alfresco Books*
7 Pineways, Appleton, Warrington, WA4 5EJ

A CIP record of this book is available from the British Library.

ISBN 1 873727 11 9

Publisher's Note: While every effort has been made to ensure that the
information given in this book is correct the publisher does not accept
responsibility for any inaccuracy.

Typeset and Design — Jen Darling

Silhouette — Gordon Firth

Printer — MFP Design & Print

FOREWORD

by Chris Bonington

The statement that we all have our Everests is something of a cliché and yet, at the same time, there is a great deal of truth in it. I was fortunate in actually reaching the summit of Everest but I had the full use of all my limbs and the benefit of years of experience in the mountains. The challenge that I faced was considerably less than the one that Jon Amos tackled in his attempt to climb Kilimanjaro in his wheelchair.

This is a wonderful story, not only of the grit and determination of Jon, but also of the dedicated teamwork of those who accompanied him. They were comparatively inexperienced, and undoubtedly made some mistakes in trying to climb the mountain before they were fully acclimatised, but their spirit in attempting the venture, and the way they worked together, was superb.

They were doing much more than just trying to climb Kilimanjaro. Their work with the disabled in Tanzania gave a very positive benefit to many people. Jon Amos is an inspiration to us all and it is a great privilege to write the Foreword to this story of a bold and courageous undertaking.

DEDICATION

Derek and I would like to dedicate this book not only to our families and friends but also to all our sponsors, the media and well-wishers worldwide, who had faith in us. They made the expedition possible, as well as contributing to its success.

Personally, my heartfelt appreciation has to go to my wife, Lynn, and my two children, Rebecca and Robert, for the overwhelming support they gave, despite the emotional and financial strains that I created.

I must also give acknowledgement to my brother-in-law, Dave Bates, and my two good friends, John Avery and John Horseman, who cycled mile upon mile with me and my son, in order to push me to the limit and keep me sane. (There are those who would say they failed in the latter!)

Last, but definitely not least, a very big thank you to the 'team', for having faith in my 'ability', and for the insurmountable support that they gave throughout the whole project. This is also extended to all the new friends we made at the International School at Moshi, who let us enter their lives. They must have been crazy!

Jon Amos

I would also like to make a personal dedication to my wife, Mary, who not only puts up with my constant quest for the unattainable but also actively assists me in trying to attain it!

Derek Groves

CONTENTS

PREFACE

The Aim

The **Roof of Africa on Wheels** project hopes to have heightened the awareness of disability sports in 1998 — the year which celebrated fifty years of wheelchair sport. First started in 1948 by Dr Ludwig Guttmann at Stoke Mandeville Hospital, this now continues through the dedicated efforts of the British Wheelchair Sports Foundation (BWSF). It is a unique enterprise which aims to achieve personal and collective goals and to foster global friendship through sport, education and endeavour.

Objectives

To take a wheelchair athlete as high on the mountain, Kilimanjaro, as possible.

To take part in a multi-national expedition based on the stated values of friendship and endeavour.

To take part in a shared cultural, educational and technical exchange within the host country.

To extend through sport, personal and collective awareness, to exchange information and share common experiences and expertise.

To take a team into the surrounding rural areas to assist in the educational, sports development and health care programmes, as part of the expedition as a whole.

Afterwards ...

To make a documentary film and develop media coverage to raise the profile of athletes with a disability.

To write up the expedition in the form of a book.

Introduction

GREAT GABLE AND PIKE'S PEAK

It seems a lifetime ago since Jon and I first began to consider special projects in the adventure sports field as a catalyst to help us in our work, developing and raising the profile of wheelchair sports.

Jon has certainly been an inspiration to me. His boundless enthusiasm, relentless training and total focus are all attributes which set him apart and make almost anything possible. I can't think of a better role model for anyone with a disability, sportsman or woman, athlete or just human being.

We first started by looking for something to push back the parameters a bit, to expand the existence envelope, to extend the realm of the possible and to go the extra yard. But it didn't quite work out like that!

I really couldn't say from where the first idea originated. It seemed to spring full-blown into my imagination and I knew straightaway that Jon would be keen to try it. We both like chasing rainbows. It wasn't long before thought became deed and, with a little help from our friends, we assembled the equipment and a team to help Jon reach the summit of Great Gable (2949 feet) in the English Lake District — all within three months!

Little did we think then that one Summer weekend would change our lives. But soon afterwards Jon and I realised that what had started out as a fund raising gimmick could be a whole new ball game and an end unto itself. Wheelchair mountaineering had begun!

The media coverage alone raised the national awareness of the limitless goals which can be achieved by people with a disability and the money which we raised from the **Great Gable Wheelchair Ramble** in June 1996, helped to fund the Great Britain women's disabled weight lifting team to compete in the World Championships, held in Colorado Springs, USA. Jon and I were coaching the team, which proved very worthwhile as they took the gold medal and the Great Britain women's team won the World Championship title!

This area of the United States, of course, also happens to be one of the world's great mountainous regions, so after the competition was over we took ourselves off to one of the highest mountains in the area — **Pike's Peak**. Rising to over 14,000 feet, it also has the world's highest rack and pinion railway. We wanted to see how Jon would cope with the altitude and this was a good opportunity to find out.

The ascent was made on a cold, clear day in the Fall. The views from the summit were wide and awesomely spectacular and I think this was when Jon realised that he could once again contemplate doing the things he so much missed and experience the delights of mountaineering which his disability had previously denied him. No word had been spoken, yet I think we both knew that it would be onwards and upwards from then on.

It was in our hotel room in the Springs where we seriously began to plan. I have climbed and trekked all my life and had only two 'dream' peaks which I wanted to climb, not for the difficulty but because they are mountains of legend — Mount Fuji in Japan and Kilimanjaro in Tanzania.

As in all things we had to temper our ambition with our ability. Not only did we have to consider time and cost but also whether it really was viable for Jon. The last thing we wanted was to attempt a mountain, or a route on it, which would be impossible. Mount Fuji was rejected purely because it was further afield and not of the same magnitude as Kilimanjaro.

So the choice was made. 'Kili' had all the attributes we were looking for in a mountain. Rising to 19,341 feet, it is the highest free-standing mountain in the world. It is equatorial with distinct wet and dry seasons, and climatic zones which make the ascent akin to a vertical trip from the Equator to the Arctic. Last, but more important to us, was the fact that 'Kili' is a trekking peak and has more than one viable route to the top.

We knew from previous experience that it would be tough, but Jon and I are realists and we thought that, with good equipment and the right team, we could make a serious attempt on the summit. The logistics of moving across mountain terrain in a wheelchair, even a specially adapted one, demands the use of a fairly large team. Therefore, we decided to impose strict rules in order to make our attempt as close to the ethics of true mountaineering as possible and so that our efforts were not seen as some Mickey Mouse fund raising event but a serious move towards developing and expanding wheelchair mountaineering, in order to enable everybody to enjoy and experience what most of us take for granted — freedom. The freedom of the hills and the ability to wander in the world's wild places — are these really only the preserve of those of us lucky enough to be able to walk? Speaking to some who should know better, you may be excused for thinking that's so. I hope we can dispel such a selfish illusion.

KILIMANJARO

Located partly in the Amboseli Game Park, Mount Kilimanjaro at 19,341 feet (5,895 metres), is Tanzania's and Africa's highest mountain, part of the chain of the volcanoes formed along the line of the Great Rift Valley. Standing only a few degrees south of the Equator, the main massif extends over an area of some fifty miles and has three main peaks.

It was first climbed in 1889 by Dr Hans Meyer, a German geographer.

Kibo, the highest peak, appears as a smooth dome from a distance but contains a crater over one mile across. Outside the crater glaciers descend to 13,900 feet. On the south-west side Kibo is linked to Mawenzi, the second highest point, by an eroded saddle of volcanic ash.

Shira, the third and lowest peak, rises to 12,800 feet.

To ascend Kilimanjaro is akin to taking a trip from the Equator to the Arctic as it covers desert, savannah, tropical rain forest and glaciated ice fields. Above the 5,906 foot contour line the whole mountain becomes a nature reserve. The lower slopes are cultivated but above 6,500 feet these give way to a forested zone. This thick rain forest belt eventually yields to groves of heather trees and dense tussock grass, the vegetation becoming more sparse until it peters out into alpine moorland up to a height of around 14,750 feet. After this point it becomes truly alpine. In the alpine zone ground temperatures can fluctuate from 104 degrees F down to below zero at night.

In the high summit region, with great climatic changes and little rainfall, life is scarce. The southern slopes of the mountain are the most fertile, receiving rain from the south-east Trade Winds. This is home to the Wachagga tribe, who crop banana and coffee.

Rainfall is unevenly distributed throughout the year. January, February, June and July are the best climbing times and, although Kilimanjaro is known as a 'trekking' peak, any undertaking to climb it must be viewed in a serious light as a mountain of this magnitude should not be underestimated. Remember that altitude does kill and that people have died on this mountain. Success and safety **must** go hand in hand.

TEAM PROFILES

Name:	**Jon Amos**
Job:	Mountain Ascent Co-ordinator and Stills Photographer.

Jon co-ordinated all aspects of the ascent and summit bid as well as coaching and teaching in the schools, orphanages and street projects with which we were involved during the project.

Age: 39

Biography: Although paraplegic following a road traffic accident some 22 years ago, Jon has been a successful international weight lifter and coach, representing Great Britain on numerous occasions. He is now coach of the British Weightlifting Association for the Disabled, is a member of the National Association of Sports Coaches and was voted Coach of the Year in 1997 by the British Wheelchair Sports Foundation.

Ambition: ... to live life to the full, making the most of his talents, and, hopefully, to help others overcome their negative thoughts about disability.

Name: **Derek Groves**

Job: Team Leader and Biographer

Age: 43

Biography: Physical Education officer and former Paratrooper, Derek is a Great Britain coach working with athletes with disabilities. He has worked with Jon for several years at the British Wheelchair Sports Foundation in Stoke Mandeville. He is a keen mountaineer and has climbed in many countries around the world.

Ambition: ... to have the opportunity to make a difference.

Name:	**Terry Barnes** (*Sirdar* - Nepalese for Organizer of Porters)
Position:	Mountain expert. (Terry had the final say on the ascent.)
Age:	40
Biography:	A Physical Education officer , ex-Royal Marine Commando and very experienced winter mountaineer, Terry has climbed and trekked in many parts of the world.
Ambition:	... to trek in Greenland and Nepal.

Name:	**Mark Harling** *(Safi)*
Job:	Deputy Team Leader and Bush Driver.
	Mark's role was to shadow Derek and pick up on everything he missed. His skill as a driver also probably saved our lives.
Age:	29
Biography:	Physical Education Officer and ex-Royal Marine Commando. *Safi* is Swahili for 'clean' and Mark always looked as if he had just stepped out of a recruiting advert. Even in the worst conditions he always appeared 'buttoned down'!
Ambition:	... to stay *safi*.

Name:	Flt. Lt. Dr **Janet Hastle** RAF
Job:	Team Doctor
Age:	29
Biography:	Born in Holmfirth, West Yorkshire, of a climbing family, after training as a GP Janet became a doctor in the RAF.
Ambition:	... to be an expedition doctor. Ambition fulfilled, we hope!

Name:	**Peter Allwood**
Job:	Information Technology and Communications.
Age:	47
Biography:	A lecturer in Information Technology, Pete is a veritable Mr Gadgetman. If it's electric he loves it! Pete's role was to document everything and get the story onto the Internet and into other media outlets. He is also a keen hill walker.
Ambition:	... to E-mail someone from the top of Kilimanjaro!

Name:	**Barry Thompson**
Job:	Project Photographer.
Age:	Indeterminate, but as he remembers the Bay City Rollers he is a bit dated and, although he hasn't admitted to being a fan, still sports a tartan scarf in Winter.
Biography:	Barry is a lecturer in photographic art and a professional photographer who has successfully shown his work both in Britain and abroad.
Ambition:	... to be an expedition photographer.

Name:	**Jim Sowter**
Job:	As leader of the Logistics Support Group, Jim was in charge of the portage team of guides and porters on the mountain.
Age:	57
Biography:	Jim was a Principal Physical Education Officer who took early retirement in 1996. Having served in the Parachute Regiment for 18 years he now spends his time in more leisurely activities such as swimming and cycling — 80 or 90 miles a day! In the past he has made trips to the French Alps with members of the Project team and has recently spent eight weeks cycling solo around New Zealand.

Jim is currently helping to coach Great Britain's disabled weight lifting team with Jon. |
| Ambition: | ... something to do with marching bands on Cup Final day and a Salvation Army bonnet! |

Name:	**Nick Allwood**
Job:	Member of Logistics Support Group. What he lacked in experience he made up for with a phenomenal work rate.
Age:	18
Biography:	Pete's son, Nick, is an apprentice engineer, keen sportsman, sex god and beer monster — not necessarily in that order!
Ambition:	... to play a large part in *Baywatch* or a small part as one of the babes!

Name:	Cpl. **Simon Davies**
Age:	31
Job:	Member of Logistics Support Group.
Biography:	A Royal Marine Commando, a 'bit of a gymnast' and interested in most sports, Simon latterly became known as the *Big Issue*.
Ambition:	... to qualify as an ocean yacht master, or make the front cover of *GQ* or *Horse and Hound*.

Name:	Sgt. **Robbie Roberts**
Job:	Member of the Logistics Support Group
Age:	34
Biography:	A Physical Training Instructor with the Royal Marines, Robbie once held the world endurance record for abseiling (eight hours) which tells you something about him. Married to Rachel, they have two young children —Alice and Jack.
Ambition:	To reach the summit of Kilimanjaro — amongst other things!

Name:	Lt. **Conrad Trickett**
Job:	Member of the Logistics Support Group
Age:	27
Biography:	Conrad has served as an officer in the Royal Marines for seven years and spends as much time as possible climbing hills and mountains — or any variation on that theme!
Ambition:	?

Name:	**Mary Groves**
Job:	Base Camp Manager and Organiser of Fieldwork.
Age:	42
Biography:	Married to Team Leader Derek, Mary is a child-care specialist and very talented in the art of inter-personal relationships — or being able to get what she wants from anyone. She has also travelled extensively and has a wealth of experience in trekking and backpacking around the World.
Ambition:	... sadly unfulfilled, to stay 32 forever!

THE WHEELCHAIR

From Jon:

Bureaucracy we could tolerate; even the problems with Information Technology were insignificant by comparison to a disaster with the wheelchair. Improbable - yes! Impossible - no! I did everything in my power to make sure the wheelchair was tried and tested before taking it up Kilimanjaro.

Problems had started as far back as the climb up Great Gable in 1996, where an ordinary, everyday folding type of wheelchair was used. It had been supplied by Alfred Bekker, a mobility specialist from Driffield, East Yorkshire, who believes that simple is best, even to the point of insisting that ordinary wheels should be fine. It only differed from a standard wheelchair in that it had extended handles and a strengthening brace on the back, just in case added control was needed. Also, a type of skid had replaced the two front wheels, to help the chair ride over scree more easily.

It stood up to the task very well indeed on the way up the mountain, except that the spokes on the wheels took such a bashing they became loose and slightly buckled. Having been naive, if not stupid, enough not to have taken a spoke spanner with me I could only tighten them with my fingers, which at least gave some tension to the wheel. Having reached the summit of Great Gable I then became overawed by the breathtaking views and forgot to check that the wheels were okay. I paid the penalty for this on the way down, when one wheel finally cracked under the strain of it all. So, for the last mile or so, the support team had to do a 'carry home' job.

With that experience behind me it was apparent that the chair to go up Kilimanjaro would have to be built with a much stronger frame and better wheels, at the very least.

I was invited along to a National Aids for the Disabled Exhibition (NAIDEX) in London later that year, to help promote cushions for a company who had sponsored us. As the exhibition was showing all types of merchandise for people with disabilities it was an ideal opportunity to talk to the representatives of wheelchair companies from around the world

— all promoting their wheelchairs as the best on the market. I spoke to many exhibitors and explained what I had done and what I was planning to do, in the hope that one of them might be interested enough to become involved in my next expedition.

The problem was that, in some sort of patriotic way, I was trying to keep the expedition as British as possible, including the wheelchair. This was not easy as none of the British manufacturers were showing much interest, that is until I contacted Stuart Dunne, managing director of *Cyclone Wheelchairs*, who's in a wheelchair himself. He invited me to his office in Ellesmere Port, Cheshire, the following week.

At this meeting, after I'd explained what I was going to do and the publicity this should generate for people with a disability, focusing on what they can achieve, he suddenly asked, 'What exactly will you need?' I told him, 'A robust wheelchair, able to withstand a tremendous hammering, have various lifting points and a tracker attachment. The design would be stringently tested before the trip and, if necessary, have to be altered.'

The tracker is an additional mechanism attached to the front of a wheelchair, which converts it to a three-wheel handcycle with a choice of gears. The reason I wanted this was to assist me in cardio-vascular training, as ensuring a high fitness level for me was paramount. I would use it in the months leading up to the expedition to do mile upon mile of training, both on and off roads.

Stuart agreed to become a sponsor and immediately started to give me other contacts which he felt might be useful. He also suggested ways in which his company could benefit and I agreed to have one of his manufactured wheelchairs for my personal use, in order to publicise both the expedition and his wheelchairs.

We went on to discuss the actual requirements of the chair and he took some body measurements. We also talked about the problems with the wheels on Great Gable. Stuart, together with his brother, Mike, a wheelchair technician, discussed various ways of overcoming the problem. It was decided that a 24 inch diameter wheel be used, with a cross spoke of thicker gauge steel than usual. On the front of the chair would be larger, balloon

Jon and Derek on Great Gable.

Simon Davies

Dr Janet Hastle

SOME MEMBERS OF THE TEAM

Andrew Burroughs (BBC)

Robbie Roberts   Mary Groves   Pete Allwood — Gadgetman

Monday 26th January — what a way to arrive!

Practice makes perfect!

READY FOR OFF AT
MARANGU GATE

Is there a problem back there? Yes, thick mud caused by heavy rain.

THE FIRST DAY
ON THE MOUNTAIN

The porters carried enormous loads.　　*Attaching clean wheels next morning.*

type, castor wheels, replacing the skid system used on the previous chair. These, Mike felt, would ride over any obstacles we might face. Only time would tell.

It was now May 1997 and, whilst the chair for Kili was being manufactured, Stuart let me borrow a demonstration chair. So, at long last the road training began. Along with John Avery, a good friend of mine, and my twelve-year-old son Robert, I started to clock up the miles. Every day I would alternate between weights and fitness training and road work, come rain or shine. The weather did not matter; there was work to be done.

We would cover any distance, from as little as seven miles up to 33 miles, alternating the terrain. On one particular occasion my brother-in-law, Dave Bates and John Horseman, a mutual friend, accompanied Robert, John and myself on the latter route. The problem for them all was that they had to keep to my pace, which would be considerably less than their normal cycling speed because of the weight of my wheelchair and the ratio of their legs to my arm power. Their legs really suffered. Robert stayed with me for the majority of the way, whereas the other three decided to keep going on ahead, wait for me to catch up and then continue pedalling away. Although I'm sure they had a strategy for resting worked out, they all denied it!

Robert was doing really well, as this would be the longest journey he had cycled. However, a little psychology now and again didn't go amiss, and everyone told him that from the half-way mark it was all downhill. Little did we know that a six mile stretch was entirely uphill and this was after we'd already completed some 19 miles cross-country.

Shortly after the uphill struggle had begun, Robert started to question how much further it was, saying he felt unwell. I thought it was a touch of dehydration and told him to make sure he kept the fluid going in.

I assured him that it wasn't much further and we had no choice but to continue. I assured him that it would level out soon. How wrong I was. I couldn't stop on the steep gradient as it was a busy major road and getting started again would have proved very difficult, so Dave agreed to stay back with Robert as he rested. Robert later said it was Dave's excuse to grab a rest himself.

They soon caught up as my pace dropped to about three miles an hour as the gradient took its toll on my arms. The triceps were absolutely burning. For Robert it must have seemed like forever as it turned out he had tonsillitis and wasn't just making excuses. The only one who was not tired after that long hard slog was John Avery's two-year-old son, Scott, who'd ridden all the way on the back of his father's bike like a king!

The prototype chair was now ready, and none too soon, as time was running out to allow for any necessary adjustments. Derek had asked Terry Barnes to arrange a trial run in the Lake District, so we could test out the wheelchair and, just as importantly, ensure that we selected the right individuals for the support team in Tanzania. We were all to meet on the second Friday in November 1997, at a prison outdoor activity centre near Barnard Castle, where Terry worked as a prison officer, to get to know each other, then travel across to Cumbria on the Saturday.

All started well on the Saturday morning, as we travelled in convoy, until yours truly realised that he was low on fuel, so low that it didn't register on the gauge. I pulled in at the next petrol station, flashing the car in front to let them know. Unfortunately, the others continued and I was told on my mobile 'phone to follow the road we were on to our destination!

After re-fuelling we drove for mile upon mile until Dave and the two Johns, who were travelling with me, started to enquire whether I knew where I was heading. Now what a stupid question to ask, of course I did! Terry had telephoned me several times over the previous weeks to discuss the mountain for our trial and, despite his broad northern accent, I was positive it was Glen Caffrey. However, I did admit that I wasn't too sure where it was and suggested we ask someone the way.

At first no one had any ideas to offer, so I thought it best to pull into a local market and ask some people there. The first gentleman I approached just laughed and asked me to repeat the name. Then he laughed again, and so did my passengers when he said, 'Are you sure you don't mean Blencathra?'

We realised we'd reached our destination, the base of the mountain, when we saw the other cars parked on the roadside. After stopping in the nearest spot, a quarter-mile up the road, we unloaded the equipment, including the tracker, which I'd brought along in case we were to cover any long, flat stretches, and proceeded back towards the others, who were waiting patiently for us to join them.

A cold, damp weather front had started to hang over the hills, causing the air to chill. I thought this would make the trial much more of a work-out. Even as we made our way to the starting point we began to note the obvious problems with the chair, especially the lack of anchor points if we were to get into difficulties.

It was obvious from the very beginning that help was needed on the steep, lower slopes, especially as the track was only as wide as a goat track. To reach that track we first had to cross some very wet, muddy marshland, complete with stream, and on a trail narrower than the wheelchair. The trial had begun! The start was much more arduous than Great Gable and a heavy mist hung over the slopes, causing the ground to be very slippery.

Derek suggested a four-man team be harnessed to the wheelchair, in a staggered formation to enable them to walk single file up the track, which had a drop-off of some 500 feet to its immediate right. The mist had turned to persistent rain and the air had even more of a chill in it, the type that got right into the joints. This would test those who were hoping to accompany me on Kilimanjaro to the limit and give them a taste of the problems which might lie ahead.

The chair was taking a fair knocking, so we would soon see if the prediction Stuart had made about not needing spare wheels was wrong. We'd covered marsh, scree, rocks and boulders, and so far all seemed to be fine.

The whole team worked extremely hard and efficiently, none more so than Flight Lt. Dr. Janet Hastle, our only female applicant for a place on the team. Being from a family of experienced hill walkers she was not found lacking in any way and was immediately on the scene when my fingers became trapped in the spokes of the wheel. The guys had thought I was stuck on a boulder and gave one almighty pull to help me overcome the 'obstacle' and my fingers didn't take too kindly to the wrenching. They were strapped immediately, before I could even say, 'Ouch! Oh dear', or words to that effect!

We had reached the higher, grassy slopes of the mountain when Terry declared that, due to the extremely bad weather conditions, we would summit and then follow the same route back down, to ensure the safety of us all. It had originally been his intention to summit and then make the descent on the opposite side in order to give the chair and the team a good work-out. However, the conditions had ensured this had already happened!

We were starting to cross the saddle of the summit so I decided to try out the tracker system, plus a change of wheels and tyres, to see if it made any difference. There was no doubt that the third wheel on the front made negotiating obstacles easier and highlighted further adaptations that were needed, especially for stability. Several changes, some major, would have to be carried out before we left for Africa and we now only had some eleven weeks before departure. There would be little time to test any changes to the chair. I'd have to be sure I asked for everything needed and be specific to the last nut and bolt.

The third wheel had made so much difference I decided I would keep it on when we started our descent. The difference, when I encountered obstacles, was so incredible that I'd already made the conscious decision that the third wheel attachment might be of great benefit on Kilimanjaro.

The only snag with the tracker was that it was designed so that you had to crank both arms forward to move and crank backwards to brake. Simple in itself but, when going down a very steep hill, I tended to push down on the crank arms in order to keep my balance and stop myself falling out, and therefore was continually braking. This caused a stop-start effect and created havoc for those following close behind, ensuring I didn't just leap over the ledge. It prompted several calls from Mark Harling to, 'Get off the bloody brakes', with my response, 'I wish I bloody could!'

Halfway down the final steep trail the sun started to peer through the clouds and offer us a wonderful view across the hills. The timing could not have been more appropriate, as we were having difficulty keeping the chair on the narrow track. With the force of gravity against us, Conrad and the two Johns were actually over the edge to my left ensuring that I didn't disappear down the 500 foot drop! At one point I thought Conrad was going to take the quick route down himself as he lost his footing to the sound of Derek shouting, 'If you go, don't take the wheelchair with you!' Moments later Derek slipped whilst holding the chair and I couldn't resist reminding him of this, to which he replied, 'Where you go I go and where I go you go.'

With an all round team effort and many lessons learnt, we finally reached the bottom. The day had been very productive and had highlighted major changes needed in the overall design of the wheelchair and tracker system.

Back at home Dave and I wrote down the changes needed to the chair, with drawings to the exact millimetre and degrees required, before I took it back to Stuart. We also noted that the wheels had indeed buckled on Blencathra and, once again, raised our concern at not having spare wheels with us, especially as Kilimanjaro was not exactly awash with cycle repair shops.

Stuart and his brother were still adamant that we would not need spare wheels! Not totally convinced, I talked to another wheelchair distributor by the name of Kieron Slocombe, who was displaying his wares at the Wheelchair Games at Stoke Mandeville. He was managing director of the company, *Wheeltech*, who import and distribute wheelchairs for the American company, *Colours*. He had no hesitation in providing me with a set of trispoke carbon wheels and, quite amazingly, asked for nothing in return, no acknowledgement, absolutely nothing. In fact he said he would be delighted if we used them so that he could quell rumours that the wheels broke under stress.

The alterations had been passed on, down to the last detail. It was now up to *Cyclone* to get the work done, and fast, as time was of the utmost importance, with only weeks to go. A few days before Christmas the chair was ready to collect. Dave and I picked it up from Stuart at his warehouse. It was looking good; all the alterations had been done and it had a fresh lick of paint.

On arriving home Dave suggested that I put the chair and tracker away ready for the job ahead, but I wanted to try it out now that the changes had been made. John and I decided to do a trial run amongst the hills which surround the village where we both live. The trek was to be about 13 miles in total, with more than enough hills on the way. We had only travelled about three miles when I thought I'd hit a pothole as the whole chair jolted, testing my balance to the limit. The headstock of the tracker attachment had sheared right through, leaving the whole thing pressing down on my knees.

What a good decision it had been to test the chair. We would have to let Stuart know immediately. Major problem! It was Christmas and he'd gone away for a two-week break, leaving us with the problem of having to find someone who could weld aluminium. We were due to leave in a couple of weeks and we were right in the middle of the Christmas shutdown.

John found that a friend was willing to do the repair, which allowed us enough time to do a final test run. It could have been worse; it could have happened on the mountain. The wheelchair was finally ready — and not a moment too soon!

Chapter One

PREPARATION

Failure to prepare is to prepare to fail.

Sponsorship — or the lack of it

1997 was a busy time. Research into routes, the climate and the best time of year to make the attempt, all ate into our time. It was going to be a bigger job of organisation than we had anticipated.

Having ascertained that the ascent hadn't been done before in a wheelchair, if we were successful it would be a world first! Good stuff. Just the thing, we thought, to get the sponsors' cheque books out. How wrong we were.

We were so naive. After finding a sponsor to supply promotional brochures, we sent out the first 500 begging letters to outdoor clothing and equipment manufacturers, car companies, the shakers and movers in finance houses and the captains of industry. We should have spent the money on our kids! The cheque books mostly remained firmly closed, although we were overwhelmed by the expressions of goodwill which poured in — sadly cashless. For those who did help, even in the smallest way, our thanks. You know who you are and your names can be found in the Appendix.

The British Wheelchair Sports Foundation was celebrating its 50th Anniversary in 1998 and we used their good name blatantly and unashamedly throughout the project. I hope we made them proud.

We never did hit the jackpot with a major sponsor, so once again we turned to our own resources and pestered, bribed and generally haunted our friends, families and colleagues to help us raise the money to make it possible. And to you all we really do say a big thank you. Without you we would never have got off the ground.

From Jon: I think they all wished we'd taken up fishing, but if we had it would probably have been up the head waters of the Orinoco!

Portage

We knew that the rules we'd set would make the attempt harder but we also knew that if we hired 50 porters to cook and carry for us, and generally just threw money at the scheme , we would not be taken seriously. We decided that all the team, apart from Jon, would carry their own equipment on the mountain. This included food and water for at least two days. With fuel and stoves this meant that each of us would carry at least 35 pounds per man — the equivalent weight of a porter's load.

We also decided that we would only use a guide (who doesn't load carry), an assistant guide and four porters to carry Jon's personal gear, spares for the chair, their own food and equipment, and the team's medical pack. We also ensured that all the team were self-sufficient on the mountain — cooking and cleaning for themselves. The only reason that Jon didn't load carry was that, to date, we haven't been able to devise a suitable method which is practical over the terrain. But we are working on it!

These self-imposed limitations came back to haunt us later but we still feel that it was, and is, the right thing to do. And in the end it lent credibility to our summit bid and, by doing so, we occupied the moral, as well as the geographical, high ground.

The Wheelchair
The World Games for the Disabled, which were held at Stoke Mandeville in the Summer of 1997, proved to be a productive breeding ground for our plans and we used our contacts in wheelchair sports blatantly, for which I do not apologise as we will probably do exactly the same again!

We collared Stuart Dunne, the Managing Director of *Cyclone Wheelchairs*, and bade him build a chair to our specifications and one which would stand up to the assault on Kili, with one overriding consideration — it had to be done for free! It turned out to be a long and costly job but it all worked out well in the end — thanks Stu!

The Team
Time was beginning to lay its hand on us. By now it was late Summer and we planned to leave for Africa in mid-January 1998. With barely seven months to get the team and all the myriad logistics in place, we had to crack on! Jon and I were the only certainties and that wasn't going to get us anywhere. So we started to approach people we knew who not only had the

requisite skills but could also get the time off work and were willing to pay for the privilege of joining us on the trip. We had to have a mix of competent mountaineers, 'tech heads' and a good logistics support team. As a Physical Education officer in the Prison Service, and with military service in the parachute regiment, I knew that by approaching the Armed Services we might get all we were looking for in a one-stop shop which, as it turned out, proved to be right.

The early team applicants were whittled down, one way or another, leaving us with a core team of specialists, which is just what we needed. We had a couple of false starts and then managed to organise a team training weekend at the Services outdoor centre at Deerbolt. This was organised and run by our good friend and travelling companion, Terry Barnes.

Terry is one of those people who are always there for you, quietly in the background, competent, capable and steady as a rock! I hoped that Terry would join us as the climb's leader and act as the Sirdar (Nepalese for organiser of porters) during the mountain phase. I need not have worried, Barney wasn't about to let us go off without him on this trip! This was good news. He would be a major asset and fill a very important role in the project. We were very relieved to have him on board.

In early November Barney organised a training session on Blencathra, in the Lake District. The weather was terrible so it gave the prospective team a good work-out under realistic conditions. This also proved to be an invaluable aid when it came to making the final choice for the team, as we were able to get a clear idea of people's strengths and weaknesses, and see how people worked together and gelled as a team.

After this weekend the team was almost in place and Jon and I felt that we had chosen people with the right attributes for the venture to be a success.

More about Money
At this point Royal Mail was still considering sponsoring the whole trip, but eventually withdrew leaving us to fall back on our own resources. Personally I felt that, although we were likely to be short of money, at least we were free agents and did not have to meet any demands or restrictions which may have been placed upon us by a sponsor. So perhaps it was a

blessing in disguise as we now 'owned' our own expedition and were only answerable to each other. We probably should have known better than to put our faith in corporations but we had to find the money from somewhere.

In the end every team member put up at least £500 of his/her own money, and some considerably more. Although it cost us all a lot of cash at least it was ours and it was a good feeling to be in control of our own destiny. However, I must admit that I experienced more than one sleepless night, wondering just how we were going to manage financially.

The run-up to Christmas 1997 was a bit of a nightmare as, at this point, we encountered a bit of a hiatus when nothing happened at all, when it seemed as if all our contacts had dried up and nobody was out there who wanted to have anything at all to do with a man in a wheelchair trying to ascend Kilimanjaro. Every 'phone call seemed to generate another knock back. I was beginning to have serious misgivings and to question our ability to get the expedition off the ground.

Christmas came and went, and I can only assume that the season of goodwill had affected people's spirits, for the tide began to turn in our favour. By late December things had started to move, much to my relief, but only just in time. Finally, it looked as if the trip would go ahead.

The Flights
Alliance Air (a subsidiary of *South African Airlines*) agreed to fly the team out at cost and to transport fifty kilos of equipment per person — free. This was a major boost to both our finances and our morale. The pressure was off, the expedition was on!

Equipment
This was being brought from far and wide, begged or borrowed, it was pouring in. Now we had the tools to work with, Jon and I were confident that we could mount a serious attempt on the summit.

From Jon: We still didn't have the chair anywhere near finished, but it was looking good and all the modifications had been made which we wanted incorporating into the design. The team was also shaping up well and everyone was making progress.

Surfing the Internet

We were even more pleased when Dave Lynch offered us pages on his *Blue Dome* website on the Internet. We now had worldwide publicity! It wasn't long before we started to get 'hits' on the site from people who just wanted to know what it was all about and also from companies who wanted to sponsor us, either in cash or kind. Technology in sport has arrived!

At last we were being taken seriously and our sponsors (and would-be sponsors) realised that we were in a position to generate worldwide interest through the media. Attitudes and positions miraculously began to change. We suddenly became a commodity! Thanks Dave, for having enough faith in the venture to give us the initial break into the media market.

Working as a Team

Christmas over, the time factor really began to tell. There was never enough time in the day to get everything that needed doing done. The team which we had brought together now proved its worth. Without their support the whole idea would have disintegrated. But the others involved just gave, gave and kept on giving.

Because of the team's efforts and the extra publicity we now started to see a trickle of money into the funds — and not a moment too soon. None of us is what you might call rich and we needed at least 5,000 dollars just to get onto the mountain. However, we were all committed to the project by now and just had to find the wherewithal to pull it off.

The International School at Moshi

Our contacts at the International School in Moshi, Glen and Debbie Canterford, were invaluable to us throughout the whole venture. Their local knowledge and contacts helped considerably with our planning and preparation. These were people we had never met, and only knew from exchanged letters and brief telephone conversations, yet they took on board many hours of work and organisation on our behalf, enabling us to function effectively during our time in Tanzania. To them, and to Phil, Jane, Kate and Sandra, many, many thanks. You made it what it was and we can't thank you enough for your kindness and unselfish competence in your dealings with us often lost souls.

Chapter Two

WE'RE OFF!

Sunday 18th January — The Day of Departure

Finally, the day dawned and the advance party of Jon, Mark, Peter, Derek and Mary met at London Heathrow's Terminal Two, to start the epic trip and, hopefully, make a dream or two come true!

After nearly two years of planning we made it with only ten tent pegs adrift, this oversight being rectified by Mark at his own expense of £1.29. Peter, Mark, Mary and I all travelled to London together, courtesy of my Governor in the Prison Service, who kindly supplied a driver and transport for us and the team's equipment .

The drive down to Heathrow was uneventful but on the way into the airport we picked up a large rivet in one of the back tyres. We managed to nurse the vehicle to the terminal entrance before it finally gave up the ghost and the wheel had to be changed. Leadership (apparently) being about delegation, I delegated Mark, who would be our bush driver in Africa, to do this. (And so did everyone else.) Unfortunately, the poor lad started the trip with a shiner as he dropped the spare wheel and caught it with his face! This proved to be the start of Mark's troubles with anything on wheels.

The last to arrive was Jon, with Lynn and the kids to see him off. We got off to a good start when *Alliance Air* gave us a priority check-in facility to help smooth our passage onto the plane, together with about 20 boxes of assorted equipment. However, although we gathered everything together at the allotted place ready to go, unfortunately the airline computer couldn't cope. What followed could be described as a logistical nightmare and eventually they just gave up and shoved everything through. The plane was only half full anyway.

The Flight

The flight was great and the air crew really looked after us. We travelled to Kilimanjaro from London via Entebbe, a place which conjured up for me memories of a plane hijack, hostages and the daring rescue carried out by the Israelis. Our journey was far less dramatic: a runway with plenty of landing room for the 747 and the usual buildings surrounded by the African bush. There was nothing to be seen to tell of those scary days: no sinister reminders to frighten the modern traveller; no burned out aircraft; no shell-scarred buildings; nothing. I was quite disappointed! We came and left without incident and, uniquely in my experience of air travel, arrived at Kilimanjaro smack on time. And by that we were impressed!

Customs
The bit we weren't looking forward to was getting everything out of the airport and through customs. The amount of equipment in-bound was enough to make the faces of any customs' official light up with the thought of all the tax dollars it may yield. However, with a little help from a friendly American Swahili speaker and the paperwork from the Tanzanian High Commission in London, we got through without parting with a single dollar. Apparently everything was in order!

The Inevitable Rip-Off
In India it's called *baksheesh;* in Africa it's *dash*; but it all adds up to being ripped off one way or another. I can understand that we appear to be the spearhead of western capitalism and that, as compared to most locals, we are rich, but what I hate most is the casual attitude towards the rip-off — the expectation that a Westerner (or probably any visitor) is fair game and that, in things monetary, he should be exploited ruthlessly.

This was to prove one of our biggest problems when dealing with African bureaucracy at any level. The game started immediately. We didn't even get the chance to have a warm up or a few practice laps. The *bureau de change* clerk 'accidentally' short changed Mary by 20 US dollars in the first ten minutes. Fortunately, Jon sorted that out in his own inimitable way, whilst Mark and I started to gather our gear together and sort out transport to the Moshi Club. In the meantime, Peter thought all the interaction made good footage and zoomed around filming everything in sight!

We eventually ended up outside the airport, literally sitting on top of our kit to stop it being spirited away by helpful African porters, who didn't seem to realise that Moshi was all of 40 or so kilometres away and they were on foot! Eventually we got things under control and entered into patient negotiations with a truck driver. I knew we had plenty of time to barter for the best deal and wouldn't be rushed. Glen Canterford had given me some invaluable information about local prices and what we should expect to pay, and I stuck to it. We finally reached an agreement about the price, but wily Africa man wasn't about to give up that easily. No indeed!

Hands were shaken and more hands started to load the vehicle. But while Mark and I were supervising this, Mary, Jon and Peter had been gently led to a second vehicle. Now we had two trucks.

'Yes *bwhana* (boss), same price for both — 19,000 shilling each!'

'No! Everybody out!'

'But you will be more comfortable like this boss!'

'No. One truck at 19,000 shillings. We travel with the equipment.'

Sadly, reluctantly and with much grumbling, Africa man agrees. He goes into a sulk and will not help us to re-pack the gear, but sits behind the wheel. Time, apparently, is money now. With a bit of jiggling, and knees to the roof, we all get in, much to the driver's disgust. He takes off at warp factor nine and has obviously decided that the sooner he is rid of us the better!

Despite the cramped conditions our first sight of East Africa was a pleasant one. The countryside is lush and green. Hang on a minute — lush and green — when it's supposed to be the **dry** season. Brown and parched is what it's supposed to be. Just what's going on?

From Jon: Well, we're finally here which, just six days ago, seemed unlikely as I was in hospital having tests to make sure the side effects I'd been experiencing from the infamous Lariam tablet had done no permanent damage, especially to my kidneys.

It doesn't seem 18 months ago that we were sitting outside the Wasdale Head Inn in the Lake District, supping ale and celebrating the successful ascent of Great Gable, when someone suggested we might try something a bit bigger next time!

There's been a difference of opinion between Derek and myself over whether or not we should take the purpose-built skis which British

Aerospace has made for the wheelchair. Derek feels they're surplus to requirements and would just be extra baggage. I hope he's right.

It wasn't a bad overnight flight. Before landing the captain commented about the wonderful view of Kilimanjaro those sitting on the starboard side would have. Of course I wasn't.

Chapter Three

INNOCENTS ABROAD!

Monday 19th January

Everywhere we looked was verdant, burgeoning greenery and this was supposed to be the **dry** season. What was going on? El Nino was to blame, or so everyone said. Apparently the long rains just never finished and it had been unseasonably wet ever since!

Having arrived safely at the Moshi Club, we took a good look at our surroundings. Like most colonial, ex-pat clubs, it had an English bar serving beer, gin, whisky, and beef sandwiches. There was always plenty of steak to be had, which looked like beef and smelled like beef but tasted of nothing in particular. One could only assume, therefore, that it was beef!

The Club was of bungalow construction, with a large, deep verandah overlooking an uneven, but well tended, playing field, with ungeometric rugby posts at either end. The manager and native staff were helpful, polite and spoke good English — far better than our meagre ten words of Swahili. The temperature was pleasant, humid and in the high nineties.

From Jon: We sat down adjacent to a magnificent view of Kilimanjaro, but unfortunately I was too tired to take it all in by now and was just waiting to stretch out.

At this point, Peter tried to test both our 'phones. We had been concerned about the digital mobile 'phone linking up as, although we'd been led to believe that there was a GSM link, our own findings had been different. We were not too alarmed when the Nokia 9000 did not function as our sponsor, Dave Watkins of the Carphone Warehouse, felt it was a shot in the dark. However, we were very surprised to find no link on the satellite telephone. We hoped it was just a minor blip.

Even at this early stage it was obvious that both Derek and Mark had a problem with modern technology and, with hindsight, this should have been sorted out then.

After off-loading our kit and stowing it on the verandah, the first, cold bottles of *Safari* lager went gratefully down our throats. We had arrived! Despite having been paid, the driver still made a show of hovering around and eventually asked if there was a tip! 'Yes' was the answer and I bought him a bottle of *Fanta*. After his performance at the airport it was the most I was prepared to do.

Debbie, from the International School, had arranged to meet us at the Club but had not yet arrived. We were quickly to learn about 'African time', which is distinctly different from central European time or Greenwich Mean Time. 'African time' is very flexible and not easy to define. 'Soon' can mean almost instantly or at an indeterminate future date! As most Africans don't own watches it is almost impossible to organise anything in a European timescale. You have to learn to be flexible and say, 'Come in the morning' or 'Be here tomorrow', to have any chance of success.

Obviously, after seven years in Tanzania Debbie had acquired some of the local habits, flexible time being one of them. We did the only thing you can do in the circumstances, made ourselves comfortable and ordered more cold beer! The driver left in a huff and we never saw him again.

The cloud continued to build up to and beyond midday. As the temperature rose so did the humidity, until the air was thick with moisture. Massive thunder clouds loomed over the mountains, and from horizon to horizon there was wall-to-wall cloud.

Finally, at around two in the afternoon, two jeeps came trailing dust down the track to the Club. Debbie arrived in a rush with her mate, Sandra. They broke over us like a storm. With introductions flying amidst ceaseless chatter and banter, it was like an unexpected meeting of old friends. They then went into top gear, organising where we were to stay, throwing in and discarding ideas and suggestions like small children with old toys. All we had to do was try to keep up!

From Jon, up on the verandah: 'Thanks then, just leave me here.'
Debbie to Derek: 'Are you going to help him down the steps?'
Derek: Don't be silly, he'll take care of himself.'
And of course I then had to, wheelchair and all.

Debbie and Sandra soon had us organised and on our way. They had decided that our equipment wouldn't be secure at the Moshi Club, so we should make our base area in a friend's garden. Phil Hudson was head of the primary section of the International School at Moshi. He wouldn't mind, they said, as his wife, Celia, a Columbian lady, was away visiting her family in South America for a month.

Phil's bungalow was down one of the dirt tracks which criss-cross the suburbs of Moshi, about a ten minute walk from the International School campus and a five minute drive from the Club. The house had an extensive garden of about half-an-acre, which was full of mature trees and bushes with grass in between, and was surrounded by a tall, thorn hedge with a double gate let into it.

We soon had the tents up and the rest of the stores stacked on the bungalow's deep verandah. And not a moment too soon, as the heavens opened and we were treated to the equatorial rainstorm which had been threatening for most of the day. We sat on the porch and watched the track to the house turn to mud and the ruts disappear into a stream bed. I couldn't help but have a twinge of apprehension at the violence of the storm and the effect it was having on the ground. Jon and I both knew how much more difficult it was for him to move around in his wheelchair in thick mud, even with the tracker attachment.

The rain lasted for the rest of the afternoon, but by early evening it gradually dwindled away and finally died out, leaving a beautiful, clear sky and a warm, westerly sun. Debbie had gone off to tell Phil that he had house guests and Sandra had gone to collect some drinking water for us. As the water supply at Phil's was unsafe all drinking water had to be brought down from the borehole on the International School's campus.

I was a bit concerned about how Phil would react to the prospect of finding the five of us camped in his garden on his return from work, even though he had been primed by Debbie. As it turned out I needn't have worried. Not long after the rain stopped a mud-encrusted, white 4x4 came slithering through the gates and pulled up in front of the house. A swarthy, muscular man of about forty climbed down and made his way across to us.

Originally from Walsall (and still with a trace of the accent) Phil had, it transpired, travelled and worked in many countries around the world and had been in Tanzania for about three years. Extremely self reliant and unflappable, he was totally unfazed by having us descend on him out of the blue. Indeed he even seemed happy to see us! His first reaction was to offer us a cold beer from his fridge. It only seemed polite to accept with gratitude.

Phil was so laid back I couldn't believe it. He immediately offered Jon the use of his spare bedroom and all of us the free run of his house. He told us that, as he would be working at the school most of the time, we could just come and go as we pleased, so long as we remembered to lock up behind us! We started off being staggered by his generosity; we were all dazzled by it before we left!

From Jon: The use of Phil's spare bed was a godsend as the new air mattress I'd bought wouldn't inflate.

Then, at a pre-set time in the evening, a satellite 'phone call from Lynn told us that the original code had been changed, which also solved the problem of why the satellite 'phone wasn't working for us.

Phil decided that, as a welcoming treat, he would take us to a roadside eating house a few miles away to sample some local cuisine. I now know what became of the Khe San runway after the Vietcong finished shelling it. They sold it to the Tanzanians who used it for the Boma road! Three miles of cratered tarmac negotiated at speed in the dark is an experience none of us will forget!

Driving along this stretch of road became known by us all as the Wacky Races. Nobody drives in a straight line, they just weave in and out of the holes, generally as fast as possible and on occasion leaving the road altogether if the going looks better alongside the tarmac rather than on it. No rules of the road apply. You can overtake on either side and in any direction. At night the fear factor increases considerably as not all the vehicles using the road have lights which work! Disneyland would do well to look at it as a prospective white knuckle ride in one of their theme parks!

Phil, who was by now used to the local driving conditions and had adapted to them, drove with one hand on the steering wheel and half turned round to talk to us. He seemed totally unconcerned and at ease, whilst we sweated and gripped the seats.

We eventually arrived unscathed at a large hut set back amongst the trees at the side of the road. Two or three tables stood in front, in a dirt yard. There were no lights outside, only the glow cast by bare bulbs hanging inside. Negotiating our way carefully to a table near the door, we sat down. The proprietor came out and wiped off the table with a rag he produced from the pocket of his trousers. He appeared to know Phil and bade us welcome — *Jambo* in Swahili.

Phil told us that this place served a local delicacy of chicken and plantain banana that we really should try. He ordered for us all then, with cold beer all round, we waited in eager anticipation for our first taste of Tanzanian food. It took a while but we used the time to get to know each other. The cold beer and easy conversation beneath a warm, velvety African sky, ablaze with stars, seemed a good start.

The chicken and bananas finally arrived and proved to be surprisingly good. The chicken had been roasted and cut up into cubes, bone and all, and was served with a mound of roasted plantains, fresh limes and salt. The plantains had a wonderful, nutty flavour and a firm texture. It was so good we decided to order the whole lot again! The proprietor was well pleased and brought out a basin and a jug of hot water so that we could wash our hands, all the better to enjoy our second helpings!

We ate and talked far into the night. It had been a long and very interesting first day but none of us seemed overtired. We eventually returned to Phil's house in the small hours. The return trip in the land rover did not seem so fraught this time.

On our return to the tents we were met by the Askari guard, who patrolled the compound at night. He was muffled up in a large worn overcoat and sported an outsize, woollen hat. Phil said that the Askari consider it cold at night when the temperature drops to around 60°f!

The night was alive with noise, considerably more than the day. We all stood quietly gazing up at the brilliant night sky, drinking in the beauty of it. Then, having said our good nights, we crawled into our sleeping bags. But not for long, the Askari might think it cold, but fresh out from the UK it was far too hot for us to sleep inside our mountain bags. I for one just lay on top gently oozing sweat until I was rocked to sleep by the lullaby sounds of the African night.

I had only just reached the edge of sleep when all hell appeared to break loose — howling, baying and barking as if all the hounds of hell had gathered around the compound. Phil's dog, Maluka (Spanish for ugly), was standing bristling right outside our tent, adding her voice to the cacophony of sound ripping the night apart. It sounded to us as if a pack of wild dogs had caught and killed something nearby and were tearing it to pieces and arguing over the kill. This went on until dawn started to lighten the eastern sky, after which it petered out into the distance. We were to be treated to this disturbing, night-time experience several times during our stay.

Tuesday 20th January
Soon afterwards cockerels began to crow and herald the new day, and we never did get a lie-in as Phil came calling at about 6.30. The battery on his 4x4 was flat, could we give him a bump start? We dragged ouselves out to the front of the house. The only way we could move the truck was in reverse with us all shoving on the bull bars. Fortunately, it kicked up first time.

As he sat there revving the engine we asked if he'd heard the commotion during the night. What was it? Had it disturbed him? Straight-faced, he said he'd never heard a thing! We couldn't believe it! Then he shot off up the track in a cloud of dust. To this day he maintains he can sleep right through the noise and never be disturbed. He must be having us on!

As we were already up we decided we might as well start sorting out the rest of the equipment and generally get organised. Brews and breakfast soon appeared — ration pack sausage, beans and porridge. Nice! We rebuilt the Tracker, after extricating it from its transit packaging, then Jon gave it a spin around the garden and proclaimed it fit to use.

He then went off to help Pete set up the satellite telephone and laptop computer we had brought out with us. We had arranged to keep in touch with various BBC radio stations, update them on our progress and, hopefully, conduct interviews, both live and recorded, all the way to the top. Pete also had the responsibility of updating information on the Internet daily in the form of a diary.

From Jon: Today Pete met Jayne Lund at the International School and she offered us the use of the laptop at her home. Without any GSM link for the Nokia 9000 this proved to be a godsend.

Mary, Mark and I took ourselves off on a local reconnaissance mission to find out what fresh food could be bought and from where. We had arranged to meet Debbie and Sandra at the school shortly after noon, to be taken to the coffee shop in downtown Moshi for lunch. Everyone in the school staffroom seemed to know who we were, but Debbie introduced us each in turn to the staff and, finally, to Geoff Lloyd, the headmaster — a tall, distinguished gentleman with a firm handshake and a ready smile.

Geoff gladly accepted our offer of help with the teaching programme and reciprocated by offering his assistance to ensure the project's success. He was as good as his word. On our way out of the school grounds we had our first good look at the mountain. It is truly beautiful, rising majestically out of the surrounding Masai steppe country, with the midday sun illuminating the high glaciers and snowfields which crown the summit.

The weather was perfect. By lunchtime, no visible sign of yesterday's torrential rain remained, only the beautiful lush greenery. Yet I could see that what had fallen as rain on the steppe had fallen as snow on the mountain. The snowcap was lying thick and low, down to some 15,000 feet — not good. The idea of negotiating deep powder high up did not thrill me.

Over lunch Debbie and Sandra recounted bad news stories from people recently on the mountain, telling of bad weather, washed out trails and deep snow — all of which we didn't want. One thing we knew for sure was that we couldn't wait long for an improvement as we were burdened with a tight time schedule, which could not be extended. Whatever the weather, come the day we would make our attempt and, once on the mountain, we would keep going for as long and as high as we were physically able. Worrying about it now was pointless; we were here and would have to take what the mountain gave. Good, bad or indifferent, we couldn't change the weather!

During the afternoon, Seamus Brice Bennett came down from Marangu and invited Mark and I to go up to the hotel which he and his family run at Marangu Gate. The Brice Bennetts are well known in East Africa, having lived and worked there for many years. The family now runs safaris and treks from the hotel and provide guides and porters for the Marangu route up the mountain. Seamus, with his family and staff, were to provide invaluable information and support for us, as well as our porters and guides for the mountain.

We arranged to meet the next day, Wednesday, for lunch at the hotel and Seamus would then help us to organise the permits and plan for the ascent. We were eager for a closer look at the mountain and tried to put the thought of bad weather behind us. Things were looking up! Everyone was bending over backwards to help us. We were going to be OK!

That evening we got time for a swim in the school pool, a real and unexpected luxury, before meeting Debbie at her house. Strange but true, it was cheaper to eat at local restaurants than to buy food in and cook it oneself! We could, of course, always fall back on the boil-in-the-bag military rations we had brought out with us, but had already decided to spare ourselves that 'pleasure' for as long as possible. The prospect of three weeks on nothing but 'rat packs' was not a source of great joy to any of us.

In and around Moshi there are a number of eateries. All are cheap. Some are better than others. On this occasion we tried out *The Buffalo*. A favourite watering hole for ex-pat Europeans, it had the usual ubiquitous steak and chips, accompanied by Kilimanjaro beer — gassy but good when ice cold — *baridi* in Swahili. I set myself the target of learning two new words a day to try to improve my communication skills, a trick which I picked up many moons ago and a good one to employ when travelling.

Many of the teachers from the school were there and we ended up with quite a crowd round us, several more tables having been added by the time we had finished our meal! There was a very mixed bag of nationalities but all were equally enthusiastic about what we planned to do — many asking if they could help in any way. The generosity we encountered everywhere was amazing. During the meal it rained again and the drive back was another exciting interlude, but we were getting used to the rutted and muddy roads now.

From Jon: Down came the rain, in torrents, making the ground a quagmire too wet for the wheelchair. I would have to use the tracker.

Tanzania is a country of real contrasts. Not primitive in the way that India is but more of a high-tech, low-tech difference. The International School at Moshi is very well equipped, with a computer room which would not be out of place in the UK. Yet the village schools have few books and often no sports equipment.

Mark and I went into Moshi to change some of the expedition's dollars into shillings and found that we were getting at least forty shillings more to the pound than we got at the airport. (You can also get a better exchange rate when changing high denomination notes rather than low ones.)

We also sorted out the team's transport with an agent Debbie had recommended. The owner and driver, Hasnain Akber Kermali, proved to be one of our most valuable and reliable contacts throughout the trip. Hasnain understood 'English time' and proved it by always being punctual. His vehicle was in good mechanical shape, clean and well maintained. Small, stocky and somewhat taciturn, 'Has' sorted out all our transport problems for the rest of the trip.

Wednesday 21st January
Today, Mark and I drove up to Marangu to see Seamus and, hopefully, to get our mountain permits, whilst Jon, Mary and Pete sorted out our contacts at the base camp, plus the hundred-and-one other tasks they had to do to ensure we would be ready by the time the rest of the team arrived.

From Jon: Using the laptop, Pete and I set up the communication system with the press, the media and e-mail links back home. It was a slow process, but then this was Africa.

Marangu appeared to us to be rather a grand place for a trekking lodge, with a very acceptable bar set amidst lovely gardens and an almost Tyrolean restaurant, in which Seamus treated us to lunch. During this we had a very useful talk about the route, the weather, the hows and whys and wherefores.

Seamus then went off to 'phone through to Marangu Gate, to contact the warden there, a Mr Moirana, who Seamus said was a good fellow. He would see us right now if we cared to drive up. So, without further ado, we said goodbye to Seamus and whizzed up the trail to Marangu Gate.

The entrance to the park and the mountain trail is marked by a large car park and a group of well-made, Norwegian style chalets, which house the Gate's administration buildings and mountain rescue post. Mr Moirana is obviously an important person in the TANAPA (Tanzanian National Parks). Everyone treated him with extreme deference, including us.

He listened very attentively to what we had to say and then gave us the bad news. The daily park fees had gone up from the 15 dollars per man per day, quoted by the High Commission back in England, to 25 dollars per man per day! This was the fee just to be in the park . He also explained a very nasty rule change. Camping was now no longer allowed. This was a real body blow as all our planning was geared towards an easy ascent, camping between the huts and taking eight days to the summit. My heart sank. This was real trouble.

Then he hit us with the killer. It would cost us 40 dollars per person per night to use the huts, plus a compulsory rescue fee of 20 dollars per person on top. My mental arithmetic isn't brilliant but I knew we hadn't got that kind of money in the kitty.

We pleaded our case long and hard, and Mr Moirana listened most sympathetically but the outcome was the same, he didn't have the authority to waive any of the fees. The best he could do was to give us two days grace in which we could lobby the director in Arusha, at TANAPA headquarters. He would hold our hut spaces open until Friday morning. If he hadn't heard from us by then, regrettably he would have to let them go.

Two sad people made the drive back to break the bad news to the rest of the team. Money (or lack of it) being always our prime concern we sat over our evening meal and had a long debate. We hadn't come this far to fall at the first hurdle. We worked out the figures and the arithmetic told us that we could not put the team on the ground for eight days as planned but we could, if we pooled all our resources, attempt the route in five days.

We would contact the rest of the team in the UK and get them to bring out all the spare cash they could lay their hands on. But first, a drive to the TANAPA headquarters in Arusha, to plead our case before the Director, was necessary, with the hope that he would make a reduction for us. Otherwise, it was going to cost us over 4,000 US dollars to be on the mountain for just five days.

I also realised, which Jon, Mark and Pete did not, what this would mean in terms of the extra work-rate and debilitation. At this stage I thought it politic to keep my own council, as morale had been damaged enough without my burdening them with my own doubts and fears.

That evening Pete and Jon made contact with our UK base via the satellite telephone and passed on the words of woe. We were all glad to hear the positive support we were getting from the home team. It cheered us up to know that the wheels were in motion and we could go on.

On the plus side, during our absence at Marangu, Mary, Pete and Jon had been to visit the Mkombozi Street Kids Project run by Kate McAlpine. We looked at the uncut film on the digicam and the visit had obviously been a real success. The kids followed Jon around like the Pied Piper! We all agreed that the film would cut up into a very good presentation piece. The others had really enjoyed getting amongst the children and had, until our return, been having a good day.

*From Jon: We conducted a satellite link-up with Whitehouse Primary School, where my wife teaches in England. Sally, a colleague married to a Tanzanian, speaks Swahili and was able to talk to the boys at the Project. Never having even seen a telephone before, some thought a person was hidden inside the handset! Seeing the excitement, joy and disbelief on the boys' faces was proof enough that IT **does** have its uses!*

'Why no girls?' I asked Kate McAlpine, to be told that girls found on the streets, even as young as five, would be utilised for prostitution. It turned my stomach.

At the end of our visit the boys sang us an impromptu song. It was the first time Kate had heard them sing since the scheme started in April 1997 and we felt honoured.

The pre-planning now, of course, would take longer than expected and kept Mark and I out of the other project work more than we would have liked. But that's why we had the advance party I suppose, although we did feel we were missing out.

On the lighter side, we invited Phil to join us for a meal and introduced him to the delights of military boil-in-the-bag rations — an experience he was curiously unenthusiastic about repeating. How strange!

Thursday 22nd January
A beautiful, clear blue African dawn greeted us and the mountain was visible. The snow line seemed to be higher — or maybe that was just wishful thinking on our part.

We had to make the journey to the TANAPA headquarters in Arusha today to see what, if anything, could be done to reduce the cost of being on the mountain. The warden at Marangu had made us an appointment to see the director, Mr Biguruube. This would be the last throw of the dice. If he wouldn't help we would have to rework our finances yet again.

Jon, Mark and I all went, mostly to support one another rather than anything else. We armed ourselves with all the official papers we could muster, as we thought these might prove useful to demonstrate our intent and that our project was officially recognised by both their High Commission and our organisation in the UK. All that remained to be done was to convince the man himself and we would be in business.

The TANAPA headquarters are based on the sixth floor of the impressive AICC building in down-town Arusha, next door to the heavily guarded court building in which Rwandan war criminals are prosecuted.

Having made the appointment, Mr Biguruube could not see us but his assistant, James, would. We told him everything, emphasising especially how much world-wide media attention Tanzania could expect to gain from allowing us on the mountain for the eight days, so that we could make a proper attempt on the summit, with the best chance of success. We showed him the pages from our website on the Internet and explained how thousands of people could access the information, and how it would enhance TANAPA's international reputation if they were magnanimous enough to waive some of the fees.

James listened with interest to our sales pitch. He seemed genuinely impressed and decided that we were a worthy cause but, sadly, he did not have the authority to waive any of the fees, only the Director General could do that. James was a nice bloke and I think he was embarrassed by the fact that no-one else in the organisation had any real executive authority. The whole thing was run rather like a dictatorship, with all the real power in the hands of just one man. James said he would explain the situation to Mr Biguruube but he could not say what the outcome might be.

He was gone for the best part of an hour, leaving us to speculate on what the great man might do. He returned triumphant, his face wreathed in smiles. He had done it. He had got Mr Big to waive the fees. We could barely keep the silly grins off our faces. This was great. James would radio the warden at Marangu and inform him of the decision **and** he would come up himself to see us off and make sure we had no problems.

After much handshaking and expressions of goodwill the official letter was produced and handed over to Jon. Jon's smile began to fade as he read it. I could see something was wrong. He passed the letter over to me. James' smile had become fixed. What was wrong? 'Mr Big had waived the fees. Everything is good, no?' Mr Big had indeed waived the fees — Jon's fees. Everyone else still had to pay. After all that effort and goodwill amongst the troops Mr Big had sent our morale into freefall once again.

James was abject in his apologies. He had done his best and dare not return to ask on our behalf again. He daren't even ask if Mr Biguruube would see us now to plead our own case. We asked if we could speak to him on the 'phone. 'No, no,' said James. 'He has left the building. He cannot be contacted. He's on his way to the Wildlife Management Centre in the bush out beyond Moshi.' We thanked James. I felt sorry for him rather than angry. He was genuinely fearful of the consequences of pleading our case for a second time. We, on the other hand, with our ingrained British attitudes, had no such scruples. We decided that we would go to the Wildlife Management Centre and beard him there! One way or another Jon wanted to speak to this man face to face.

Not being very smart we took off across the bush in hot pursuit! After blazing a trail across East Africa we finally caught up with Mr Biguruube at the Centre, about twenty miles into the bush up some of the worst trails we had yet encountered. He was not best pleased to see us. Trusting Jon's powers of persuasion we let him do the talking. Mr B. didn't want to know anything at all. He wasn't the least bit interested in our exploits or the media or anything we thought we had to offer. 'Be grateful I have waived the fees for Mr Amos. Now clear off.' Message received and understood Mr B.

The waiver would save us about 400 US dollars, for which I was grateful, but we would be stretched very thin financially and, worst of all, we would now definitely have to make the attempt in five days. Not good! However, now the decision had been made for us it was easier to accept. No more speculation. We had a fixed timescale and there was nothing we could do to change it. The one plus out of all this was that we would not have to carry tents. This at least would help us make the pace.

Up in three and down in two — Mr Moirana thinks we're mad! He regales us with stories of doctors who came out from Scotland, having spent time trying to acclimatise by using a hyperbaric chamber before they came out. (Used for recompression or decompression, this sealed chamber provides a high pressure environment to relieve the symptons of pressure-related diseases and other medical conditions.) His laughter at this bizarre episode seemed to sum up his thoughts about the British, 'All mad, the lot of you!' Well, maybe he's right.

I paid the deposit on the huts and the peak fee, the balance to be paid on the day we set out, in cash in US dollars. That done it was a bit of a relief. We now knew we had a place in the huts and the permit to allow our attempt on the mountain. All the months of planning and preparation finally came down to one, small, flimsy sheet of paper. It all seemed real then. I knew we were going up the mountain and I knew we would all be out to give it our very best shot, regardless of the odds. The challenge was before us; we only had to accept it.

That evening we went out to dinner with a crowd from the International School. Pete and Mary had been working there all day, organising the sports equipment for distribution to the project's various locations. It wasn't until we arrived that they realised they'd booked us into a rooftop restaurant! Debbie was particularly horrified, thinking that Jon would be offended. She hadn't yet realised how much Jon likes to show off his ability to tackle these little difficulties! 'Two flights of stairs. Is that all. No problem.' And it wasn't. We enjoyed a very ordinary meal of pork chops and chips, eaten under a canopy of stars in the warm African night.

Comments to Jon on arrival at the rooftop restaurant:
Debbie: 'Take it as a compliment that I forgot your wheelchair.'

Derek: '*We've come to Africa to go up a mountain, so if a few steps cause a problem we're in serious trouble!'*

From Jon: Sitting at the table's end, I kept flicking away from my neck what I thought was dust falling from the overhead canopy, until Debbie screamed, then told me it was a Nairobi fly which, if squashed, produces an acid which leaves a serious burn. Later, Phil also told me of the Mango fly, which lays its eggs in damp washing. These then transfer onto the human body and eat inwards. All towels and clothes have to be ironed. It makes the mosquito seem almost tame!

During our scheduled satellite link-up that evening we were told that the BBC's World Service was going to follow the climb.

Chapter Four

PROJECT WORK AND FINAL PREPARATIONS

Phil Hudson extended his hospitality still further by inviting the five of us in the advance party (Jon, Mary, Mark, Pete and I) to stay with him for the rest of our time in Tanzania! Such exceptional generosity is hard to credit. I couldn't envisage people doing the same in the UK. Jon slept in Phil's spare bedroom, amongst all the expedition equipment, which was much better for him as, by being comfortable at base, he would be that much fitter for the climb. The rest of us were in our tents in the garden. The best bit is that we can cook properly in Phil's kitchen and use his shower. Luxury!

The people we met in the school and local community went out of their way to help us and, without them, we would have struggled. Debbie volunteered to put up the main party in the grounds of her bungalow on the school campus, where they will have access to clean water and, best of all, the gym's showers. I think they were pleasantly surprised.

Friday 23rd January

This turned out to be an easy day — a pleasant change as it was the first day since we arrived that we hadn't put in 14 hours hard graft. Mark gave a presentation at the International School, showing the pupils our rations and stoves. He also cooked them some of the boil-in-the-bag food. Pete went along to film the episode, which turned out to be very entertaining!

Mark set up the petrol stove and arranged his demonstration material on a desk at the front of the classroom. Talking the kids through what he was doing in his best instructional manner, he stepped up and ignited the stove. Whoof! A three-foot column of burning petrol erupted from the jets. He certainly captured his audience's attention. The kids loved it ! Mark never batted an eyelid. He calmly told them that this was a graphic illustration of why one should never use a stove inside a tent! We were impressed!

When he finally got the thing under control he cooked up a mess of dumplings in butterscotch sauce. We all considered them to be inedible so we had loads to spare! These, he was about to unleash onto his poor, unsuspecting victims in the classroom. Now whether it was the novelty of being allowed to eat in class, or whether children's taste buds are different from adults, we'll never know, but they downed the lot in two minutes flat. And one brave little Oliver Twist even asked for more!

From Jon: Another live link-up to Sally's class in England, this time with Debbie's class at the International School. It worked extrmely well, especially as Debbie taught students from all parts of the globe. Interesting questions were asked by both classes, even though the schools are far apart in terms of resources and social class.

I then toured the school with Debbie to see how it could be made more accessible for a student in a wheelchair.

The rest of the day we lazed around the garden. The weather had improved. It hadn't rained for a couple of days and the tracks had baked into rock hard ridges where the 4x4s had driven over them. *Safi* was really getting the hang of bush driving, negotiating the Khe San runway on the Boma road like a veteran. Debbie lent us her 4x4 Toyota to run around in and Hasnain would provide the other vehicle to bring the rest of the team in on Monday. All the logistics were in place to receive them and the rest of the equipment.

We had a good discussion session whilst we relaxed and made sure we 'were all singing from the same hymn sheet'. The dollar situation was our main concern and would remain the critical element throughout. Jon and I, as the organisers, decided we would not see the expedition fail through lack of funding and would pool our resources, putting all our personal money into the pot. Mark and Mary also gave what they could and we ended up better off by over 1,000 US dollars. With the extra money coming out with the team we knew we should have at least enough to scrape by, even if we spent the last week with nothing but 'rat packs' to eat.

Jon was quite tired. He hadn't spared himself at all during the run-up to the mountain phase. I wanted him to be fully fit for the hill but it was no good me telling him to slow down and take it easy. He's his own man and will not quit if he thinks there's work to be done which he should be doing.

I wanted to reduce the commitments on Monday and Tuesday to a bare minimum, so that the team could gather itself, relax and get sorted out ready

*Mandara to Horombo— definitely **not** a nice day!*

This says it all.

The track was rarely wide enough.

After Horombo — this was better.

We made it to Kibo in good time.

*Jon lets rip on his unsupported
descent across the plateau.*

Ready for the summit.

FOILED BY THE WEATHER

A safe return to the last watering point.

It's still hard work, even on the descent.

A bar and a beer — what a bonus!

Our loyal, cheerful, hardworking porters.

for the hill. I knew we would all be required to make a big physical effort and I wanted us all to be ready for it.

From Jon: Tonight, I shared my body with a hungry 'mossie'. It left me bites in awkward places, which I then had to watch carefully in case they became pressure sores.

And on the satellite link-up I learnt that my son, Robert, was doing his usual, 'Dad's away, have problem', routine, this time by picking up an injury in a rugby match.

Saturday 24th January

The weather remained settled, dry and very hot. Mark and I took a class for baseball out on the playing fields at the International School and it was nearly melt-down time. We managed to get half-an-hour in the school swimming pool afterwards, which was a much needed relief and a real treat. Jon joined us and we had the pool to ourselves. There can be few outdoor swimming venues to match it for location.

During the afternoon Mary and Phil went to one of the National Parks near Arusha and Mount Meru, to film the wildlife. Phil, with some of his colleagues from the International School, had been up at the Ngorongoro Crater two weeks previously. Their video footage showed us a landscape awash with water; the tracks completely washed out. Even the old African hands had found the going tough and told us they could not remember a season like it. They reckoned that when it started to dry out and turn to mud it would be impossible to get into the area at all. Debbie wants to organise a safari up to the Tarangire, to catch the wildlife at the waterhole at dawn. I hope we get a chance to do that.

Mary worked hard setting up contacts locally at the Mkombozi Street Kids Project, the Kishari Orphanage and local schools. She and Josiah, the Tanzanian coordinator for the local Community Aid Scheme (CAS), distributed the sports equipment which we had brought out, to the most needy places. Some of the local schools do not run PE programmes because they have no equipment whatsoever — no bats or balls — nothing. We took all the sweets from the 'rat packs' for Mary to give to the kids. Some of them had never tasted chocolate. Mary came back most days emotionally drained by what she had seen, but cannot help because the problems are so big and our resources so small.

Pete had a bit of a disaster with the satellite 'phone when it got drowned with an unexpected burst of water from a conduit whilst he was transmitting. This is not recommended and it went off line and refused to function. Pete was despondent. Jon was upset. Mark and I got into real trouble for being insensitive and laughing. Losing the communication system was serious but not life-threatening. Jon and Pete spent many hours trying to dry it out and get it to function again, but it remained dead .There is a lesson here for the manufacturers. The system is good and the technology works but it needs to be more robust — and waterproof.

From Jon ... You just have to sit back and imagine the scene. We were out in the middle of an open playing field adjacent to the school, on what had to be about the hottest day of the whole project. The sun was high and strong, but we had found ourselves a convenient spot of shade, under a small avenue of trees which separated two playing fields.

Pete had just set up the satellite 'phone ready for our next scheduled talk to the media at large. Within seconds of shouting, 'Great, we've got a brilliant signal', and as if by military precision, Conrad rang through to ensure all was fine at our end and we were all ready for the rest of the team to arrive. Pete had just finished telling him of our bureaucracy problems when the disaster happened.

We'd been coaching baseball to the boarding students and a few were fooling around whilst awaiting their turn to bat. One student began to play with a water hose which, unbeknown to us, had been propped up on a tree, presumably to be used for irrigation, when suddenly water shot everywhere, including straight at the satellite 'phone. Pete moved like a rocket but still water managed to splash onto the receiver. It really was over and out! Phrases such as 'What if?' and 'If only ...' filled our minds but our main concern was what our sponsor, Chris Woods of Applied Satellite Technology, would think and would he believe our bizarre tale of water from nowhere? Also, what would we now do about the media coverage we'd set up?

Derek and Mark just stood and laughed—so at least someone was happy!

The BBC finally made a commitment to send out a cameraman to film the ascent. Andrew Burroughs, from the News team, was to fly out with the rest of the group, arriving on Monday. I had mixed feelings about the media. I didn't want the whole thing turned into a circus, with us being expected to perform for the camera. Yet we needed the media if we were to promote our work and raise the profile of disability sport. However, when we started upwards there was to be no going back for retakes. I made it plain that we would not tolerate that kind of interference. The camera was to record what took place not dictate what happened. The logistics needed careful handling.

Seamus organised our guides and porters, who would be waiting for us at his trekking lodge on Wednesday morning. We would be going with a guide, an assistant guide and four porters. These would carry the spare parts for the chair, our food and fuel. We were to carry everything else we needed ourselves. Hasain was to transport us to the Marangu Gate, then return to the Lodge to pick up our porters and bring them up to join us. I hoped the weather would stay as it was — perfect!

The loss of the satellite telephone has meant that we were reliant on the ordinary telephone system and e-mail to get our stories out. We informed our radio contacts and made arrangements for them to 'phone us to do live broadcasts and recorded interviews. Jon was still upset that we wouldn"t be able to transmit a blow-by-blow account from the mountain. I must admit that I was not all that upset. Personally, I would have preferred to go up the hill, then send out the information afterwards. All this intrusive technology offended my aesthetic awareness.

Sunday 25th January
Mark, Mary and I went to check out the arrangements for locating the rest of the team today. It was only about a five minute walk from Phil's and close to the amenities on campus. Jane, one of the teachers, had offered to put on a 'welcome' meal for all the team and some of the school staff. Brave woman, but this was just another example of the amazing hospitality extended to us throughout our trip.

Mary, Pete and Jon went off to the foothills of Mount Meru, near Arusha, with the GSM ground station equipment, to try to make contact with our

UK base. They were hoping to have a SIM card sent out (whatever that is). They thought re-initialising it would make the satellite 'phone live again. All this was like Star Trek to me.

From Jon: We found no-one capable of repairing the unit and no GSM digital coverage, which was not surprising when we discovered the satellite system operated here was bought from the French ten years ago.

We also needed a break from Derek, who would make no attempt to understand the importance of media coverage on a trip like this and was very stressed about the money situation. However, on the up-beat side, we had donated over £3,000 in equipment and resources to the projects with which we were involved and had also completed a heavy work schedule.

Mark and I spent the bulk of the day sorting out our personal gear and the kit that we should have to carry for Pete and Jon on the mountain, so that they could concentrate on filming. The rest of the gang would be arriving tomorrow morning, on the weekly Alliance air flight that we had come in on last week. Only a week had passed, yet it felt as if we had been there much longer. Phase Two was about to begin. We were ready and the weather, although more cloudy, remained good. With temperatures in the high nineties, itwas humid but so far there was no rain.

Monday 26th January

From Jon: An e-mail reported good news. The Sunday Times, The People and the Daily Telegraph were all following our progress, making all the PR work worthwhile.

I then visited the kindergarten at the International School, talking to the older students about a book they were studying, 'Whose Life is it Anyhow'? Some interesting points were raised, although some of them seemed to think I was a character in the book!

Mark and I made an early start this morning to pick up the rest of the team from the airport in Debbie's truck. Hasain would meet us there at nine o'clock. The Alliance air flight was once again bang on time. What an airline! The 747 really looked impressive as it came in to land, the big bird kicking up dust all the way down the strip, then taxiing back to the control buildings. There are no jet ways at 'Kili' just the wheel out steps, so we were able to see everybody dismount and make their way to the terminal.

Pete had come along to film the arrival and disappeared into the duty free zone. We waited for about half-an-hour before he came out to say they were having a spot of bother with customs! Why wasn't I surprised? I was called through to speak to the officials. The problem, it seemed, was the rations. Why were they bringing food into Tanzania? There is plenty of food in Tanzania. Yes, indeed there is! I had to think of something quickly as they wanted to charge us £200 in tax! I stood in front of the official's desk like a schoolboy and was made to wait until he and his accomplices had worked out the best method of extracting money from the situation.

A large ledger and a calculator was produced, pages were turned and numbers punched several times until they appeared satisfied with the result. A figure was conjured up — 109,000 Tanzanian shillings! How, I asked, had they arrived at that figure? At what rate was the duty being levied and on what had they based their calculations? I was glared at and further discussion took place in Swahili. I was glared at some more, then was told I must pay for the food. I agreed, but not 109,000 shillings. The food itself wasn't worth that much. More Swahili and pointed looks, before I was asked how much I was prepared to pay! After a bit of negotiation I agreed to pay 100 US dollars and was duly given the all-important, official papers. We were free to leave. I couldn't wait, having got very fed-up with all this bureaucratic rip-off.

We loaded up both trucks, this time without any hassle from the local porters. I think Hasain had read them the riot act and sent them all packing. With the new arrivals enjoying the local sights on the journey, we had gone about half-way when our truck suddenly lurched to the left and started fish-tailing all over the place, accompanied by the most horrendous metallic screeching. Mark, who was driving, did a magnificent job, keeping control and bringing us to a halt still upright and on the road. We got out to see what had gone wrong. The back, near-side wheel had come adrift, shearing the axle, the brake pipe and everything else, before wedging itself under the wheel arch! Travelling at over fifty miles per hour in a fully loaded vehicle, the five of us could count ourselves lucky we all walked away unscathed.

We ended up leaving five of the lads behind with the truck and what equipment we couldn't cram onto the second truck. Hasain then deposited us all safely at Debbie's bungalow on the International School's campus. She thought I was pulling her leg about her vehicle and it took some time before she accepted that we had killed it!

There are only two, tow trucks in this part of Tanzania — one in Moshi, the other in Arusha. So I guess we were lucky to get one at all. It was arranged that I should meet the truck at the International School and escort it to the broken-down vehicle. Phil, being his usual imperturbable self, just gave me the keys for his Isuzu Trooper and bade me go and recover my team!

The tow truck, when it arrived, turned out to be a hundred-year-old land rover, chopped down and converted into a breakdown truck by having a towing hoist welded onto the cross members under the flat bed. It was fitted out with a hand-cranked winch, had wheels which wobbled and only one headlamp. All in all it looked in far worse nick than the vehicle they had come to rescue.

The crew were a real Fred Karno's Army too. The gaffer appeared to be an old black Moslem with a filthy beaded prayer cap, a dilapidated roll-up stuck to his lip and no teeth. His mate was tall and round, with tattered shorts which reached below his knees, red rubber flip-flops and a vest which was as black as he was. These two were accompanied by three little boys who hung off the upper body like monkeys! Even though it appeared to be a bit of a circus these guys knew what they were about and soon had the truck hoisted and ready to go. The final problem was the fact that Debbie's steering lock didn't work. So the driver's mate just jumped in and steered whilst being towed backwards! The tow back to the repair shop on the Koreloni road cost 35,000 shillings (about £30) — not bad considering the distance and towing difficulty.

The team settled into their new surroundings as you would expect from men as experienced as these. Jane's 'welcome' meal turned out to be a real feast, with home-made pizza, lasagne, curries, ice cream, biscuits and lots of cold soda and beer! Magnificent! The newcomers didn't last beyond nine o'clock. I guess they must have been tired!

Chapter Five

THE ASCENT

'The time has come, the walrus said, to speak of many things.' And so we did. Our final briefing and general discussion took place on Debbie's stoep (Afrikaans for verandah.) Everyone was a little tense. We all knew now that we had a real battle on our hands. No-one had any illusions about how physically demanding the climb was going to be and we all had questions to ask ourselves. Three days up and two days down was a task that would test us to the limit, both physically and mentally.

Jon was gathering himself mentally for what lay ahead. He, more than any of us, had something to prove. He'd made a singular commitment to the project and had in many ways **become** the project. Having made a public statement of his intent to climb this mountain, it would be on Jon that the media spotlight would fall, win or lose, and I knew what it meant to him.

DAY ONE   MARANGU TO MANDARA
Wednesday 28th January
All our personal equipment and the porters' loads had been prepared and moved up to our pick-up point at the International School. Hasain would meet us there and move us up to our starting point at the Marangu Gate. It had to be an early start as we had to climb up to the Mandara hut before nightfall and we wanted time to get ourselves organised and the team shaken out into some kind of order. Once again we managed to cram the whole team, plus our equipment, into and on top of Hasain's truck, for the hour long ride up to Marangu. Cramped limbs and sweaty bodies are the **real** African experience!

After leaving Moshi by the Koreloni road we started to climb across the long, outflung spur of Kilimanjaro, heading north. As we climbed, the vegetation started to change and we saw baobabs — that unmistakable and uniquely African tree which looks like giant, prehistoric celery! Savannah also began to give way to cultivated areas of coffee and plantain plantations, the whole landscape becoming more lush as we gained altitude. As we headed on up towards the cloud base it began to rain. After several days of dry, sunny weather, we were almost surprised. But then we are heading into the rain forest belt.

We stopped off just short of the Marangu Gate, at the Brice Bennett's trekking lodge, where we were introduced to our guide and porters by Dominic Brice Bennett, who explained to them in Swahili the purpose of our trip and that Jon would be in a wheelchair. A rate per day was agreed and hands shaken. Dominic then explained to them that we would send the vehicle back to pick them up after we had sorted out the payment for our permits with the authorities at Mandara. Andrew Burroughs, the BBC cameraman, and his porters, would accompany them. An up-front payment was made to our guide to enable him to buy food for the porters, which consisted mainly of *mealie* meal from which they produced the ubiquitous *ugali*, which they ate for breakfast, dinner and tea throughout the trip. On arrival at Mandara the heavens opened and we were once again treated to the full force of a tropical downpour.

It took about an hour and two false starts before we managed to get our permit and our guide signed on. I tried to explain to the guide that we wanted to go up the supply route, which our information said was a wide track used by land rovers to supply the huts. It wasn't until days later, on our descent, that we realised this route didn't run through Mandara at all.

Marangu to the Mandara hut, at something over 9,000 feet, is reached by a trail running through the rain forest belt. The continuous rains had badly eroded the trail leaving it deeply gullied, with tree roots exposed in the trail bed. Add to this the thick glutinous mud, and water running down the track, and you get some idea of the problems we faced. The track was not quite wide enough for the chair, which meant that Jon was continually being thrown off balance to left or right, as first one wheel then the other drove up the gully walls. This was bad for Jon and exasperating for the rest of us as we continually slipped and fell trying to keep out of his way.

From Jon: The heavy rain had caused a clay slick to come flooding down the hill, so that the chair, its wheels solid with soft clay, looked like a dumper truck from a building site. It was also hard enough coping with tree roots, rocks and bracken without the extra burden of the clay which, as it started to dry out, made the wheels much more difficult to turn. I also thought the gears might have seized up.

The team, however, was in good form. Buoyed up by the fact that we were on our way at last, they just threw themselves up the route with no thought of tomorrow, or the amount of energy they were expending, It took the best part of seven hours to cover what was a five hour amble at trekking pace and without loads. We were wet through and muddy on our arrival at Mandara, but happy to be there and, although it had taken a while for us to sort ourselves out, we were working well together and beginning to gel as a team. We had made reasonable time and were optimistic.

From Jon: By the time we reached Mandara I was desperate for the toilet —one of my major concerns on the whole expedition, for obvious reasons. I had been told that there would only be the stand-and-squat toilets but here the ladies had the luxury of a sit-down loo, of which I took full advantage.

Meanwhile, Robbie had removed the wheels from the chair and washed the clay off under the outside tap.

The Mandara hut, or rather the one we were in, was the usual basic type which we are used to in Britain, with rough, wooden bunks lining the walls, tables and benches in between and battery powered lights. At this stage we hadn't yet developed a camp routine and kept getting in each other's way, which produced flashes of temper. But we quickly sorted ourselves out and set about our personal tasks. While Jon organised his bed space I made us our first mountain meal and a big 'wet', as the Marines refer to a brew. Once this was done night and cloud had fallen around us, and the temperature was on its way down. So we did the only sensible thing and retired into the old down cocoons for the night. Deep joy!

I had gone off almost as soon as I had warmed up the bag and was well into the second round with Melinda Messenger when I was rudely interrupted by what sounded like someone loudly packing their rucksack! There were lots of rustlings and scraping noises all emanating from under the nearby table. Jon had heard the commotion as well and, sticking his head out of his bag, demanded to know, 'What the xxx monkey's interfering with my kit?'

It turned out that the hut's rat was helping itself to the part-eaten rations which had been slung into the trash bag under the table. A well aimed boot sent our unwelcome guest on its way. This little drama became known as 'The Saga of the Rat Pack Monkey' and was retold with many embellishments throughout the trip and beyond.

I had just settled down again and was trying to find my way back to Miss Messenger after this little nocturnal episode when Barney came steaming through the hut in nothing but his purple North Cape underwear and boots, slammed the door and disappeared off into the night, presumably to answer an urgent call of nature. I decided to put Melinda on hold until Barney had made the return trip. So much for a quiet night!

DAY TWO   MANDARA TO HOROMBO
Thursday 29th January

The day dawned dry but claggy, with low cloud enveloping us in a dank, dreary fog which swirled through the forest trees and around the huts. No dawn chorus greeted us today. According to the route markers it was a five hour trek from Mandara to Horombo. We had all day so I wasn't unduly concerned about the extra time it would take us. We had expected to over-run the trekking times by a good margin and I wanted to go as slowly as possible to conserve the team's energy for when I needed them higher on the mountain.

After about an hour on the trail we started to leave the rain forest behind and broke out into the savannah, which consisted of sage brush, gorse and heather. We expected the trail to improve over this section but what we found threw a shadow on my heart. (And the Lord said to Derek, 'Smile for things could be worse'. And so I smiled and lo things did get worse, very much worse.)

The terrain we now found ourselves in was hell for Jon in the chair and for the support team. The rain had exposed all the sage brush stumps from when the trail had first been cleared. These were about the size of a baby's head and were dispersed unevenly all across the trail bed, with rocks and boulders in between. The bush was still too thick on either side for us to go cross country, so there was nothing for it other than to endure.

From Jon: This brought back memories of the impressive book, 'Bicycles up Kilimanjaro', but at least bikes could be carried when necessary! Running into a sage bush stump hidden by tussock grass was just like hitting a brick wall and, together with boulders, bracken and river crossings in steep-sided gullies, the workload was horrendous for everyone.

This type of trail was almost impossible for Jon and he required the assistance of the support team now just to keep moving. We could not find any rhythm and life was a head down struggle as we tackled obstacle after obstacle. We would roll out for about 10 to 15 feet and then have to stop and get the poles in to lift the stuck wheelchair for the same distance again, time after time, on and on. The weather too began to deteriorate and a cold rain blew in over the saddle from the north, turning the ground underfoot to mud. We were not having a nice day!

Then one of the strangest things happened. We were overtaken by a mountain guide by the name of August Juma, who had been sent out to find us. He was carrying a letter addressed to me, from Joe, Kate's mountain guide husband, with whom we had become friends. Joe worked the Machame route on the mountain and, knowing that our communication equipment had broken down, had sent August to find us — with a radio!

It was one of the MAF sets, which August could operate, and he would carry this for us from hut to hut so that we could contact MAF headquarters and they would get our messages out for us. We were so grateful to these men for their thoughtfulness and the effort they had made on our behalf.

August carried the radio and all his own equipment all the way to the Kibo hut, over 15,000 feet, then all the way back to Marangu Gate, and asked us for nothing. The radio enabled us to contact Mary back at base camp, which proved to be very fortuitous in the end. So August Juma shot off to Horombo to establish our radio link and we soldiered on.

That horrific day we also crossed seven, deep rocky gullies and made seven river crossings, having to lose and then regain height each time. The day wore on and we wore out. The final climb out from the last gully to the Horombo hut was made on head torches in the dark. We had been working solidly for over twelve hours.

Andrew Burroughs was waiting to film our arrival and had set up his lights pointing straight into our eyes. So we couldn't see a thing as we scrambled the last few yards to the huts and some caustic remarks were hurled his way as the team was totally exhausted with the day's efforts and a sense of humour failure had set in, in a big way!

From Jon: As with the first day I didn't see much scenery, being too busy trying to spot the best route. The final gully was perhaps the worst. Very tentatively we made our way into it, on a track barely wide enough for a walker and with Robbie perched on the edge of a ten-foot sheer drop to my left, just to keep the wheelchair from tumbling into the churning river.

As luck would have it we were booked into the upstairs section of the communal hut. I'd had enough at this point and being carried up a narrow staircase was more than I wanted to face after the twelve hour slog. However, we managed to change to a hut with only three small steps.

There were no toilet problems today either. Cutting a hole in the wheelchair's spare seat canvas provided a very useful, makeshift loo and the hut even provided some privacy.

As we settled into our huts it began to snow — the perfect end to a perfect day! The wind picked up too and the temperature plummeted. Jon and I ran over our options and came to a decision. We called the team together for a briefing before we all turned in, and laid out the game plan. I began by pointing out the obvious: it was taking far too long to cover the ground and the team was debilitating faster than we could recover. So we were presented with a situation of diminishing returns.

It was now snowing heavily and we were only just over 12,000 feet — not good. The last water point lay on the plateau between Mawenzi and Kibo, at around 14,000 feet. This meant increased loads as we would have to carry enough water to last us from there to the summit and back to the water point before we could replenish our vital water supplies. Everyone would need to carry a minimum of at least five litres of water if we hoped to make it to the summit.

DAY THREE   HOROMBO TO KIBO
Friday 30th January

I decided on an early start and, if the trail did not improve and we didn't make the last water by midday, then I would call a halt and turn back. This was not greeted with enthusiasm by many of the crew, including Jon, but the hard calls had to be made and it was my job to make them. I know that many of the team did not know what was waiting for them at the higher altitudes and, to be short of water and as tired as they now were, things were going to be tough and get tougher.

After such a long and exhausting day even the hardest men were feeling the strain and I was worried that more than one of the team was already beginning to show the first signs of altitude sickness. This had obviously been exacerbated by the speed of the ascent, coupled with the extremely hard work and load carrying.

We had agreed that, to make the attempt viable, we had to impose rules on ourselves so that we could not be accused of sensationalism and success at all costs. To this end we had elected to carry loads equal to, or in excess of, the porters' loads of 35 pounds per man. In addition to looking after ourselves on the mountain, and carrying and cooking our own food, we had agreed that we would not make use of any drugs to alleviate the effects of altitude until we became so debilitated that our doctor ordered their use and we had to retreat to lower altitudes to recover.

Because we were not allowed to camp between huts the tents had been left back at base camp so if things went wrong for us as we got higher there was no bolt-hole, no escape into the safety of a tent. We had to be able to make the distance or risk being caught out in the open in a weakened state, possibly with people debilitated severely by altitude. I know that people can die like that, even on a so-called trekking peak, and we were not about to let that happen. That night in the huts of Horombo we slept the sleep of exhaustion rather than that of restful recuperation, and woke with bodies not recovered from our previous labours. This was make or break time.

As luck, or the gods of the mountain would have it, today started under clear, hot, blue skies with no wind. The trail out of Horombo was steep and rocky but not as bad as we had encountered on the previous two days. After the initial climb out of Horombo we were faced with a steep, rocky ridge about 300 feet high and perhaps a mile in length. This made us dance the high altitude slow jig as we panted, gasped and swore our way to the top. After this only a couple of shallow spurs stood between us and the saddle between Mawenzi and Kibo.

This high plateau of volcanic debris reminded me greatly of Iceland — a barren landscape of volcanic ash, totally devoid of vegetation. In a dip in the ground we came to the last water point on the mountain — a weak, spreading trickle seeping away into the dusty landscape. From here the track disappeared into the heat haze at a steady incline for several miles and produced the best going on the entire route, but in a temperature of about 100°.

Pete Allwood had been suffering, along with our stills photographer Barry Thompson, and both were now finding it a real challenge just to keep going. We would try to get them up to the Kibo hut and then they could be settled down with Diamox to gather themselves for the descent.

After a couple of miles Andrew Burroughs also became ill with severe altitude sickness and was almost delirious by the time our doctor got to him. Janet decided that the only course of action was to get him back down to Horombo, or even lower, for him to recover. This was a situation I had anticipated but did not want to happen. One of our guides was dispatched to take Andrew back down safely, together with Janet, who lost valuable time treating him, then had to catch up with the rest of the team where she should have been.

Janet made outstanding efforts during this part of the ascent and her work rate was phenomenal. The whole group now started to work together well and a superb team spirit developed, with everyone supporting one another and every action being made as a cohesive unit. We knew then that these people were all made of the right stuff and would go the extra mile.

At this point Jon and I realised that we would lose the entire film crew for the summit bid. Pete was being sick every few minutes and Barry had gone quite funky and was having a hard time even communicating coherently.

Almost everyone else was OK and doing well. Although very tired we hauled into the Kibo hut at around four o'clock in the afternoon, after a cracking run across the saddle.

From Jon: I was a bit disappointed at this point, by the lack of extra speed from the chair. Perhaps the clay had got into the nexus hub or the wheels hadn't been oiled after washing, but the gears felt as if they were stuck in top gear. Whatever, I would have to battle on.

On our final stretch up to Kibo we had the unforgettable support of fellow climbers, some on their way down, others, like us, about to attempt the summit. Their applause was heartening.

After a short rest I sent out Robbie Roberts to reconnoitre the route ahead so that he could brief us on our chances of getting Jon to the summit. Robbie, our Marine PE instructor, proved his worth that day. He 'recced' the route almost to the crater rim and was back in one-and-a-half hours, having gone well above the 17,000 foot mark. With only four hours rest I would ask him to go out and do it again on the summit bid, with the rest of the team.

Robbie reported that the track was passable and the decision was made to go for it! We would leave at midnight, after just six hours rest and less for Robbie. Brews were made, Pete and Barry were given *Diamox* and everyone tried to get some rest. With the night came the cold and, after our exertions that day, I lay and listened to the laboured breathing of the others as they lay sleeping around me.

All too soon I knew we would be called and that we would have to make the final all-out effort to reach the summit. If determination alone could carry us to the top we would be there already, but we had to do it the hard way and fight for every foot of altitude if we stood any chance of success. I also knew that I couldn't afford to lose even one more team member on the summit bid as I would then run out of team and could not spare the people to look after and take down anyone who succumbed to overwork or the altitude. We were committed but we were on the thin edge. Each of us was about to be tested.

Chapter Six

SUMMIT BID AND DEVILISH DESCENT

Mad dogs and Englishmen go out on the midnight run!

Physically, our bodies were running to stand still. The few precious hours of rest had not worked any magic. I lay awake listening to the sound of the team breathing, dragging in long, ragged breaths and sighing exhalations in the cold dark. I don't know how many managed to sleep; I just wanted to get up and get on with it. My mind and body were taut with expectation. Years of planning and effort had brought us to this point, the launch pad of our desire, the fulfilment of a dream. We stood on the thin edge, at the limit of our ability.

DAY FOUR   ONWARDS AND UPWARDS
Saturday 31st January

The witching hour arrived and we rolled out of our sacks into the early morning cold. The team shook out slowly, sorting gear and preparing themselves. There was no laughter now; talk was quiet; everyone was quietly determined.

Winford and Joseph, our two guides, showed up a few minutes later, asking if we were all alright and ready to go. They too were serious and all set; their usual fixed smiles put away. They had become so much a part of the team that I'm sure they felt they had a stake in the outcome as great as ours.

Outside the hut we got ourselves organised, roped up and everyone checked out his partner. We were using the buddy-buddy system for the summit bid, so that everyone was responsible for another person and that meant we were all watched for signs of illness or injury. Everything was ready. All the words had been said and now it was time to go.

In the glare of head torches we all looked haggard. In the inky blackness we set off up the summit track out of Kibo. The team now consisted of Jon, Janet, Barney, Jim, Robbie, Conrad, Simon, Nick, Mark and myself, with Winford breaking trail and Joseph in the rear with the wheelchair spares.

The trail began to steepen almost immediately and to zigzag sharply from side to side across the slope. The surface underfoot also became softer and looser the higher we climbed. The zigzags were so acutely angled that it became very difficult for the team to stay in touch and Jon was having real difficulty manoeuvring the chair round the tight, rising bends.

About half-an-hour out of Kibo Joseph came galloping from the back to say that Nick was missing. From what we could gather he had become ill and dropped back. Joseph had kept him in sight as he stepped off the track to vomit but either he had switched off his head torch or the battery had failed. Anyway, Nick's light had gone out and Joseph had not been able to relocate him on the vast, dark mountain side.

This was both desperate and dangerous. I didn't want the team spread out all over the mountain in the dark, so we decided that the bulk of the team would stay right where we were and that Joseph would go back with Janet in case Nick needed medical attention. We would keep our head torches on so that they could find their way back to us after they had located Nick.

As Joseph and Janet set off into the night in search of Nick, Jon and I discussed the situation. We were both very concerned for Nick's safety and we prayed that he hadn't wandered off to be lost in the vastness of the mountain. Nick was the youngest and least experienced man on the team. I couldn't help but chastise myself for not making sure a more careful watch was kept on him. With little food, not much water and suffering from altitude sickness, if he could not be found he could die on this mountain. All we could do was wait and hope.

The wait seemed interminable, but eventually we saw two lights climbing towards us out of the darkness below. Only two. I feared the worst when Joseph and Janet arrived back alone. Janet soon put us out of our misery, however, when she explained that they had quickly found Nick sitting a little way off the track. Although suffering and debilitated with altitude sickness he was otherwise unhurt, but unable to continue. They had gathered him up, rushed back down to the hut at Kibo and left him in the care of Barry and Peter, his father. Joseph and Janet had then come all the way back up to our high point to rejoin the team.

To get this far up the mountain had tested the strength and resolve of the hardest members of the team. For Janet and Joseph to have come up to this high point, returned to recover Nick and take him down to the safety of Kibo, then climbed back to the high point again as quickly as they had, was nothing short of amazing. In Royal Marine jargon they would be known as 'nails', as in 'hard as', and I for one definitely agreed with the definition.

We had lost much time and needed to press on. Our time on the summit bid was limited by logistics. We not only had to reach the summit but get back, not just to the Kibo hut, but also to the last water, which meant all the way back across the plateau at 14,000 feet. And we only had the few litres of water which we were carrying ourselves.

Now we were nine. As we laboured upwards the ground beneath our feet became even softer and looser. Every upward step we slid half a step backwards. This was not just frustrating but increasingly tiring. We decided to abandon the zigzags and try to go straight up what was now a fifty degree slope, onto the summit cone.

This was a nightmare. The focus of our existence had become the pool of light at our feet. We now all lived within a cone of light, struggling for breath, fighting to stay on our feet. The pain of our existence was within ourselves. We struggled onwards and upwards until, one by one, we broke ourselves on the unforgiving slopes. We had done our best. We had come to the end of our strength. We could go no further.

Somewhere in the region of the Hans Meyer cave we called our last halt. We were over 16,000 feet high — just how high we will never know for sure as we hadn't calibrated the altimeter on Jon's watch before our ascent.

From Jon: This major decision was made that much harder as I was feeling fine by comparison to all the others, with the exception of Janet and Robbie. However, common sense prevailed and, for the first time in my competitive life, I had to base my decision on what was best for the team and not for me as an individual. (We had just reached the snow line as well.)

Once the decision was made to turn back all that remained to be done was to shoot some film at the high point, get Jon's feelings on the matter and start back down. Jon was bitterly disappointed but philosophical. Everyone had given of their best and we couldn't have asked for more. A combination of bureaucracy, bad weather and bad luck had denied us the final accolade of the summit. Down but not out, bent but not broken, we turned our backs on the Roof of Africa for the last time.

La descente infernale is the only way to describe the next hours. With bodies and minds exhausted, and the impetus of the ascent lost, the descent through the dark towards Kibo became a kind of purgatory. As we stumbled and slipped, fell and got up, it was almost impossible to concentrate on anything other than the automatic tasks which we performed.

My only thought was to get back to Kibo and into my sleeping bag, to close my eyes and sleep, in the hope that in sleep I would find more strength. No-one was speaking now. Everyone was pulling on the last reserves of will power and energy deep within themselves, holding themselves together just as long as it would take to make it back to the hut.

Throughout the descent in those early morning hours I was beset by my own self doubt. Feelings of failure and self reproach washed over me, leaving me depressed and emotionally spent. I was the team leader and had to take the ultimate responsibility for our failure. Whatever had gone wrong would be laid at my door, and rightly so.

The character and commitment of the team had been impeccable. Jon had come through mentally and physically strong to the finish. I had let them down. I should have thought it out better, fought the bureaucrats harder. With more time on the mountain and a slower ascent we would have made the summit, of that I had no doubt. All the devils of my own self pity pursued me off the mountain that night.

From Jon: The steep climb up was now obviously sheer going down and I had to hold the brakes on the chair continually so as not to lose complete control whilst it slid fiercely down the scree slope. All of a sudden something seemed to give. The mud causing the problem with the gears on the ascent had worked free through the continual braking, the brakes had released themselves and the chair was freewheeling downhill. The rest of the descent took no time at all!

We arrived back at Kibo at about 4 am, just as the first blush of dawn started to spread across the eastern sky over Kenya. I couldn't believe we had only been gone for four hours. In that short time we had terminated our chance of success as we burned up our energy on those steep and sliding slopes.

Pete, Barry and Nick did not have to ask the outcome. We were back too soon to have been successful. The bubble had burst. We just threw our kit down and climbed fully clothed into our sleeping bags, totally exhausted. I woke up after only a couple of hours of fitful sleep. I felt awful. I knew that I was badly dehydrated and had a banging headache. I hoped that the others weren't any worse than I was or we might still be in trouble, as it would take us two or three hours to get down to the water point.

I dragged myself out of my sleeping bag and woke Jon and Mark. It was only just after 6am but I knew that it was folly to stay up here with little water. Mark and I got the stoves going and went round, waking those who were asleep, and collecting water from everyone to start a major brew. We took a half pint of tea to everybody and then got things moving again.

From Jon: We talked to a couple of other climbers, from the USA and Australia, who'd managed to get further up the mountain than we had that night. They told us that conditions were so abysmal we wouldn't have made it to the summit anyway and that many others had turned back because of the weather. At the time, I didn't feel any better for hearing that.

I wanted to get everybody focused so that no silly mistakes occurred on the descent. I knew how easy it would be for people to switch off, thinking it was all over. I needn't have worried; these guys were professional to the last. Tired as they were, they never overlooked a detail. Kit was checked and double-checked and, after a frugal breakfast, the team once again saddled up and prepared to descend.

From Jon: Before setting off I changed the wheels on the chair from the conventional spoked type to tri-core carbon in order to help Kieran Slocombe, managing director of the British company, Wheeltech, to combat rumours that this type of wheel was not suitable or sturdy enough for an active wheelchair user, and were prone to break under stress. I can only say that I had no problems whatsoever.

Jon was going to make a high speed, unsupported run across the plateau from 15,000 feet down to around 14,000 feet — a distance of three or four miles between Kibo and Mawenzi.

Pete and Barry set out first so that they would be in a position to film Jon as he made his run. There would be no retakes on this one! After Pete and Barry had about half-an-hour's start, Jon prepared to make his run. He was seriously short of water, so I gave him what I could spare of mine and we arranged to meet at the saddle above the water point, where we would all join up again for the more difficult terrain below.

Jon was totally on his own now. If he screwed up, crashed and injured himself he would have to wait until we caught up to receive any help. He was pumped up for the descent. A long, fast, high speed run without us holding him back is the kind of thing Jon relishes. He set off out of Kibo at a fairly controlled pace but, as the slope steepened and dropped away, he dropped to the low bars, hunched over and let it rip! He was cracking on at an amazing pace on the x-cores while I was making about two miles an hour. By the time I cleared the rise out of Kibo I couldn't even see him in the distance!

From Jon: With brakes and gears running freely I must have come close to the land speed record at 14,000 feet. I slowed down a touch after one of the rear wheels caught an isolated rock, shook the wheelchair from side to side and momentarily put my heart in my mouth. However, all was well and I pressed on.

The rest of the team made their own way down, at their own speed and in their own time, in small groups, in pairs or on their own. Mostly in silence, the formations came together then dissolved in an abstract way as we spread out over the landscape.

By the time I caught up with Jon I was seriously dehydrated again. With a headache like a steel band round my head, it took me a while to recover. Jon, however, thought it was a hoot and was not at all sympathetic, telling me that he had had to wait ages for me to catch up and if I couldn't do better than that he may not come out to play with me again!

By the time we reached the last, or in this case the first, water we were all in pretty poor shape and had no option but to collect the water, chuck in a couple of sterilising tablets, swill it round, then throw it down our throats.

After repeating the operation several times, we had still not slaked our raging thirsts but our bellies were full. I topped off my water bottles with powdered orange from the ration packs. This stuff is known in the army as *screech*. It is so acidic that when drunk it has that effect on you! It is totally foul and leaves the tongue and lips a day-glo orange. Its only purpose, one assumes, is to take away the taste of the sterilising tablets. And it only tastes marginally better!

From Jon: A steady amble then took us back across the saddle and, for the first time, I was able to take in the breathtaking views across the plains and relax a little in the hot sun.

On our arrival back at the huts at Horombo Jon received a spate of congratulations from other trekkers, from many nations. It surprised us to discover how many people had heard on the World Service about our attempt, and knew who he was. We had obviously made some impact!

This time around the huts felt like luxury hotels and the plentiful water supply a cornucopia! We settled down to major brews and as much food as we could eat.

At this point Jon was having some serious problems with his personai hygiene, which was really upsetting him. As he said, not being able to keep himself properly clean made him feel really disabled.

That night we crawled into our sacks and crashed. Sleep took me like a black hole and I never touched the sides.

From Jon: I had a restless night, mainly due to the horrendous snoring from the hut next door! Next morning I looked back at the snow-laden summit and promised myself that one day I would get there.

Chapter Seven

BACK TO BASE CAMP

Sunday 1st February

We awoke to a truly beautiful African dawn; an awesome panorama of gold, ochre and fiery red spread before us and washed over us. Mount Kenya posed dramatically on the far horizon, mirroring her big sister, Kilimanjaro, out across the Serengeti. Far beyond the Masai steppe the Ruwenzori hazed blue in the still dark plains — a wonderful spectacle lit by the early morning light. All around us were the soft voices of the African porters, their aromatic wood smoke blueing the air as they prepared their morning meal of *ugali*, porridge and tea. These sights and sounds will stay in our minds forever.

From Jon: At this time all I could hear was everyone exclaiming about how wonderful daybreak was. I could only take their word for it as I was once again left stranded in the hut with the wheelchair outside. Is this what being disabled means?

Looking down from our vantage point at over 12,000 feet we could see all the way back to Moshi, many miles away. That would be our final destination, beyond the rain forest across the veldt. After an earlier discussion with August Juma we'd decided to try a different descent route in order to avoid fighting our way back to Mandara through the sage brush. Memories of that terrible day supurated like a raw wound. August assured us that we could get off the mountain and down to a village called Mauau by a land rover track which should be much easier to negotiate than the trail to Mandara. We trusted his judgement and would give it a go.

With the reduction in altitude, rehydrated, rested and fed we all felt much better and were optimistic that we could make a fast run off the mountain. It was the best weather on the mountain so far: clear blue skies, no wind and warming up nicely. We unloaded all but our essential rations and distributed them amongst the porters. I'm not at all sure they fully understood about boil-in-the-bag food or that they really wanted it, but they accepted the gift graciously none-the-less.

To get on the track to Mauau we had to retrace our steps and climb out of Horombo up to the saddle — a distance of less than a mile. We all felt well and rested until it came to pulling up the first slope. Then it hit us, our legs seemed to lack any strength and our breathing immediately became difficult. I think it was at this point that we really began to understand how much the climb had taken out of us. We were once again reduced to the high altitude shuffle but this time at only 12,000 feet!

We passed the track leading down twice without it registering in our minds. How we missed it I'll never know — perhaps because it didn't feature in our original plans for the descent. However, as soon as we turned downhill things got better. The pull of gravity and the easy going had us racing down what turned out to be an easy trail with very few obstructions to slow Jon down. Dik-diks bounded away from us through the long grass and we made excellent time, dropping at a rate of over 1,000 feet every hour. The lower we descended the better we felt, so that by the time we hit 9,000 feet the air felt as thick as treacle and with every breath more energy coursed through our bodies.

Jon was having a great time! We just couldn't keep up with his speed of descent. For mile after mile he would often be alone, or with just one of us running with him on the trickier parts of the route.

From Jon: *Eventually, it was time to give the others a chance to catch up, to have a refuelling break and to rest my arms, especially my joints, which were absorbing most of the shocks of travelling across such rugged terrain.*

Finally, we left the alpine zone, with its tall grass and giant groundsel, to dive into the green twilight of the fern dripping rain forest. The trail became slimy and wetter but was still by far the best track we had been on the whole time we were on the mountain. We eventually stopped for a midday meal and a rest, but it was some time before everyone caught up.

The speed of the descent, and the angle of the slope, were knocking the hell out of my knees, while the constant pounding was pushing my toes painfully into the front of my boots, so that every step was becoming more painful. And I could see by the looks on the faces of those around me that I wasn't the only one who was suffering.

From Jon: At times I had the brakes held on under full pressure and still the wheelchair kept gliding downwards at an uncomfortable speed. My only hope was that, if the chair went over, one of the team would be able to stop me from falling out altogether.

And then the inevitable happened. Crash, over I went. My legs were strapped into the chair so that they wouldn't bounce around with all the rough movement. This had worked well until now. My hip felt as if it had popped from its socket and I had a terrific pain up and down my leg —quite amazing really as I have no feeling in my legs. Momentarily I wondered if my leg was actually broken.

However, with a hefty heave-ho, and help from Simon, I managed to get the wheelchair upright again. I'd obviously only wrenched my hip and, uncomfortable though it felt, I'd really no other choice but to continue.

As the trail became even more rugged and rutted my arms were taking a real hammering, which worsened when the ground became very wet as we approached the rain forest belt.

After several hours we broke out into plantain plantations and cultivated land. The slope eased off considerably and became the beautiful rolling steppe we had longed to reach. We knew then that our journey was nearing its end. The track soon became a dirt road and Jon was able to roll out in a much more leisurely and controlled fashion.

Before long we started to pass the odd hut with children peering at us from behind Moma's skirts as she worked in her garden. The buildings started to crowd the edge of the road and, as we neared the centre of the village, everyone came out to take a look at us. I guess they hadn't seen anyone like Jon and his wheelchair before! Having cleared the forest we noticed that the cloud had been steadily building throughout the day and now huge thunderheads were strung out from horizon to horizon. Then, as we pulled up level with the township's *pub*, the heavens opened. So, of course, we did the only sensible thing and went inside!

The pub proved to be a wooden shack with a bare earth floor and wooden benches around the walls. The *bar* was a small room behind a metal cage.

You got served through the bars! We assumed this was to deter the punters from stealing either the stock or the cash. Most local shops were built along the same lines. However, as *rich* whites we were often invited through the metal security barriers to browse through the wares, whilst their *poor* black African brothers stayed firmly locked on the outside!

Here, we were ushered into the *snug*, where we dumped our kit and gratefully accepted the beers and cokes which Frederick conjured up through the bars of the serving hatch. Bosses, guides and porters all crowded together out of the rain and toasted each other right royally!

I decided to take the opportunity of this unscheduled rest stop to pay off the porters and guides, which takes both time and patience. Even though the rate had been agreed at the outset, bonuses had to be discussed and there was endless debate about how each fellow had worked harder, carried more and been more helpful than his colleagues, and so deserved a bigger bonus! We had all been impressed by these men and I had every intention of seeing them well rewarded for their efforts on our behalf, but one must be seen to play the game and hard bargaining is respected and expected on both sides.

I would urge those of you who travel to this country and undertake a trip where you will be responsible for local labour to put away your European ways and consider the African. He lives in a land which has no Social Services' safety net for him or his family, no National Health Service or free medicine. He must work to live and provide for his family. In fact **all** the family often work, including the children, just so they can survive.

A guide gets paid less than £10 sterling per day for being on the mountain. A porter can expect about £8 per day. When there are no paying clients they don't get paid. Would you carry 35 pounds or more to a height of 20,000 feet for £10 a day just to satisfy a white man's curiosity?

The locals in the *bar* made us very welcome and soon the team was in lively debate with them. Some of the lads were invited to take some *mealie* beer — the local home brew which is a thin gruel made from fermented millet, similar to Nepalese *chang*. The whole of the Royal Marine detachment, plus some of the others on the team, readily agreed to give it a go. Those of us who had previous experience politely declined. The lads were duly handed plastic mugs of the stuff and, with a good show of bravado, slung it down their throats. It must be said that the boys showed courage in the face of adversity. Even with mouths full of mealie bits and evil scum off the top, they swallowed and said 'thank you' without batting an eyelid — a truly impressive performance and one which the locals greeted with enthusiasm by offering more *beer*. This time politely declined!

Winford, our chief guide, had not liked me paying off the men myself and was now in a sulk. I discovered the reason from Frederick, our assistant guide. The chief guide hires the porters and assistant guides and then, as their agent, takes a cut out of their wages. By paying the men myself he had missed getting his cut, hence the sulk. The rest of the porters and Frederick all thought it highly amusing to see their boss being ripped off, so much so that Frederick even bought me a beer!

The whole portage team had done a good job for us. They never complained and their work rate and load carrying was excellent. The Marines rated them all *nails* and they certainly were! On the mountain I never saw any of them take a drink and few of them ate anything between breakfast and the evening meal.

Frederick, the assistant guide, was superb. A young guy in his early twenties (he didn't know exactly how old he was) he always had a smile and was ready to turn his hand to anything. In fact, he would embarrass us when we were struggling with the work and the altitude by walking beside us with the rucksack of spares on his back, his own personal kit in a sack balanced on his head, hands in pockets and a cigarette dangling out of the corner of his mouth. Then he would smile, say 'OK' and motor on past in his flip flops — or even barefoot if it was muddy!

When we were having a nightmare on the ascent on Day Two, on the way up to Horombo, the porters went on ahead, dumped their loads and came back to help without being asked or told to do so. They were never offered, or asked for, extra pay; they just did it on their own initiative. This kind of loyalty certainly endeared them to us all and I, personally, consider that to be the true character of these men. So many Africans are chasing the almighty dollar, but up on the mountain these men showed their genuine humanity and that alone made the trip worthwhile, allowing us a glimpse of the real African.

After paying off the men we just sat back and let it all wash over us, taking in the ambience of the location, watching the tropical rain beat down then pour off the eaves. One of the old, local *gaffers* came over and engaged me in conversation, asking if I wanted a *car* to take us to Marangu. We had contacted Mary the previous night back at base camp in Moshi and asked her to arrange transport to meet us there. Having come down to Mauau we still had a twenty kilometre trek to meet up with the transport.

I asked him how many the *car* would take and he said 'all'. This was one big car! In East Africa all vehicles are *cars*, so this one could be anything from a truck to a bus. But he insisted that it could take the whole team, porters, kit — everything! Frederick volunteered to go and check it out and, if it was suitable, he would negotiate a price and meet us with it on the Marangu road.

After Frederick left we settled up with the bar owner, then once more saddled up and prepared to move out. We could not be sure that the transport would be suitable, or that Frederick could negotiate a deal with the owner, so we had to assume we would have to trek the whole way to Marangu. This time the going was easy, over good dirt roads, and we were able to swing along and make good time. Surrounded by local children, Jon looked like the Pied Piper of Hamelin as we headed out of Mauau and we gathered a rag tag band, all following our progress, with many two handed *polyhassannas* (phonetic) to Jon. Roughly translated this means, 'Your grief is mine brother' — a nice touch and truly meant.

Suddenly, a native bus appeared round a bend in the road, flashing its lights and with Frederick hanging out of the door, waving! This was our *car*. Everyone was delighted. None of us had relished the hike back to Marangu, no matter how good the road. Now that we were off the mountain we felt that everything was over and we only wanted to head back to base camp for a shower, a good feed and some sleep. My feet were in a mess from trying (unsuccessfully) to keep up with Jon during his descent. My deeply held conviction is always that a third class ride beats a first class walk every time. And I, for one, had no feelings of guilt about not finishing the whole trip on foot. I was looking forward to the ride!

The bus was of the type well known and loved throughout Africa. Painted in garish colours, a full length roof-rack welded on top and little glass in the windows, this was a beautiful bus! Willing hands helped get us and our equipment on board, then waved us off on the last part of our journey. In the UK this bus would have been scrap metal. The interior and the seats looked like they had come out of a 2nd World War bomber, the suspension was shot and the whole thing felt as if it would fall apart every time we hit a pothole, of which there were many!

The old boy driving was a great character and spent most of the time looking back over his shoulder and talking to us. He drove that bus with a passion, swinging the wheel left and right, and getting on the horn at every opportunity. He just loved to drive! It was a rough but pleasant journey, just sitting back, taking in all the sights, sounds and smells which are uniquely Africa through the open window. It seemed like a cool way to finish the trip, and all for less than £1.50 (sterling) each.

Arriving back at the Marangu Gate was like carnival time. We were immediately surrounded by a crowd of locals, who started picking up our kit as soon as it was jettisoned from the bus. It then took a deal of persuasion to stop them wandering off with it! I don't know where they thought we were going. I don't think they cared. But we finally managed to get the gear into a pile on the ground, in some kind of order.

As I was paying off the driver someone said, 'Your missus is here.' I thought it was just another wind-up so I just said, 'Yeah right'. I only realised it was true when I heard someone behind me say that Mary was here with the vehicles! I looked around and there she was, with a convoy of land rovers from the International School, with Jayne, Sandra and Josiah all sitting behind the wheels smiling at us. This was great!

Mary came over and gave me a hug and a kiss, which was a really special moment. She'd never been on a big climbing trip with me before and it was good to be able to share this moment as we came safely off the hill. We had not been sure whether Mary would have got our message about the change of route and I had planned to use the bus to run us out to Moshi if she hadn't shown up. She'd got the message from MAF headquarters alright, but then had been unable to contact our driver, Hasain, as it was a Sunday and he'd gone on a picnic with his family. So she'd gone over to Jayne's and they'd 'phoned round the International School staff on campus. And here they were, right on cue as always.

After I'd signed off the guides and porters with the Park authorities we were on our way. After five hard days on the mountain we were ready for something a little more substantial than *rat pack* food, so we stopped at the C &M grocery on the Lema road, to buy beer, bacon, eggs, sausage, fresh tomatoes and two loaves of bread.

Back at Phil's we got the tents up while Jon took a shower and Mary got the grub going. Then, by the time we had all cleaned up, supper was ready and, boy, did it go down well! We shifted the lot! By the time we'd taken the beer on board we could hardly keep our eyes open and after saying good night to Jon and Phil we collapsed into the tents and slept like the dead.

Chapter Eight

PROJECTS AND LEISURE

Monday 2nd February

Today was designated as a day off but, inevitably, we ended up with various administrative tasks which needed our attention. In the afternoon Mary, Mark and I went into Moshi to arrange transport to the airport for our departure on the following Monday. Mary also organised a one day safari to the game reserve in the Arusha National Park for Thursday. It would have been a pity not to visit at least one of the famous parks in Tanzania during our stay and Arusha was within an hour's drive.

On the shopping front, the more we delved into Moshi and its environs the more interesting were the places we unearthed. There was the genuine Asian patisserie, with a few tables and a selection of very good fresh breads, quiches and pastries. The major find, however, was a wine merchant, where we were able to buy a couple of bottles of acceptable reds at a very reasonable price. So the fresh bread and cheese, washed down by red wine, made a very agreeable repast by candlelight — Monday being power cut evening!

Jon and Pete had been invited out for a Chinese meal by some of our friends from the school, although what a Tanzanian Chinese tastes like is anyone's guess. However, Jon swears it was the real thing! We were all still suffering from varying degrees of radiation burn, fatigue and insect bites so a cosy night in the comfortable surroundings of Phil's bungalow, soothed by a glass or two of wine, was a good way to get our minds in order ready to start work on the team projects lined up for us the next day.

Tuesday 3rd February

The day dawned gloriously hot. As soon as the sun creeps above the horizon you can tell the kind of day it's going to be and this one was always going to be a scorcher! The mountain was visible and we could see the whole of the ridge line between Mawenzi and Kibo. The snowline was down low again. The storms we had heard in the evenings had obviously hit the mountain, and snow was still being dumped on the summit — very strange as this is still supposed to be the dry season. Hundaningo, Phil's housekeeper, says this is *very* bad. Although everything is lush and green, there will be a problem later as the maize crop cannot be planted because it is too wet. This could mean that the crop will fail and cause shortages later in the year, which would be disastrous for the subsistence farmers.

After breakfast we were scheduled to do a film shoot with Andrew Burroughs, who wanted to get some footage of the Tracker for background. Jon conveniently escaped to one of the local projects and told me it would be good experience for me! Andrew duly arrived and set up his camera and sound equipment. Then we went over the *take* to make sure I got it right. Unfortunately, however, I appear to be totally unphotogenic and didn't enjoy the experience of *talking to camera* all that much either. Mark and Mary found it highly amusing and sat lounging in garden chairs, snapping their books shut and shouting 'Take', until they were told to clear off.

As soon as Andrew Burroughs had completed his filming he took his leave of us and left to fly out to Dar-es-Salaam, then onwards to the UK to get his rushes out for the BBC news programmes.

Mary had organised a full programme of projects for us and was busy sorting out who needed to be where at any given time during each day. We had to make visits to the Kishari Orphanage, the Annexe for the Blind at Mwereni Primary School, the Mkombozi Street Kids Project and the **Kilimanjaro Christian Medical Centre.**

Jon, Janet, Peter, Barry and I went off to the Medical Centre, with Josiah Mchome, the International School's aid projects co-ordinator, to film Jon meeting with a quadriplegic gentleman who, because of his disability, had been confined to bed for the past 25 years. In Tanzania there are not the facilities for independent living which we enjoy in our own country.

From Jon: *INSPIRATION*
There were those who said I was an inspiration to others. I suppose that was part of the project as we wanted to show others what people with a disability can achieve.

Our turn for a ride! Local children enjoy the joke.

At the Mkombozi Street Kids Project.

AT MWERENI PRIMARY SCHOOL

Learning braille.

Building the field kitchen.

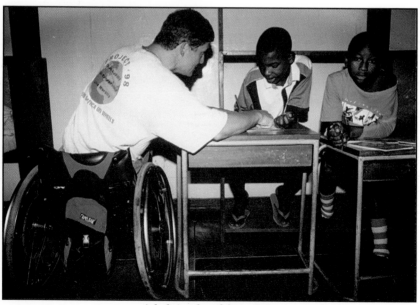

A helping hand from Jon.

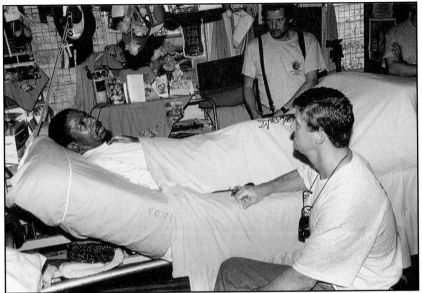

Visiting Alec, the paraplegic at KCMC hospital.

On safari in Arusha National Park.

The team on
Kilimanjaro

Voted the British
Wheelchair Sports
Foundation's 'Team
of the Year' in 1998.

We shall be back ...

Whilst at the International School at Moshi I was told of a paraplegic at the KCMC hospital who was visited regularly by some of the students at the school. They had even fund-raised to buy him a portable television set as he didn't make much effort to leave his room.

I was asked if I would go to the hospital and visit this young man, known as Alec, to try to 'inspire' him to make the effort to do more for himself. I agreed to do this after returning from the mountain and, keeping my promise, returned to the hospital with some other members of the team, including Barry and Peter, who wanted to record the visit, and Andrew Burroughs, the BBC cameraman/reporter, who felt that here was a story of human interest.

On our arrival at the hospital we had to wait for some time and were told it was because of red tape and paperwork. I was beginning to feel uneasy about this whole episode at this point, especially with the TV camera going to film the visit. Would Alec feel at ease? Was it going to be like a circus showcase? Either way I wasn't too comfortable with things in general. We were finally led to his room — camera's clicking, TV camera rolling and Andrew Burroughs climbing 'everywhere' to get the best shot. Enough was enough and I told everybody so — stop or I was out of there.

It was blatantly obvious that our wait was due to the fact that Alec had to be washed, dressed—yes! dressed—and clean bedding seen to. There he was, with two other patients whom I was told were privileged to share with Alec as he had a TV. He was pristine, including collar and tie, in this very hot, non-air conditioned room. We talked awhile. He was very literate and well educated, and exclaimed that he had hoped one day to visit England.

Bearing in mind that I was asked to encourage Alec to 'do more for himself' I'd noticed a wheelchair, of sorts, semi-covered up in the corner of the room. I say 'of sorts' as it was an old fashioned chair, with large wheels at the front and small ones at the rear — the opposite of modern chairs.

This alone would make any paraplegic think twice about attempting very much, but even more so Alec because, although I had been led to believe that he was a paraplegic, he had in fact suffered spinal cord injury at a high level, so was dependent on other people for most tasks. As with most high level tetraplegics or quadriplegics Alec had very little, if any, use in his arms, so pushing a wheelchair himself was out of the question. Awareness is definitely needed at the school.

But even with his disability Alec could still think positively as he commented that, despite his disability and lack of facility, out of a small window in his room he could see Mount Kilimanjaro every day, and for this he was thankful — a lesson to us all I think.

On returning home to England I was to be confronted by this word inspiration once more, when the headmaster of Moorlands Junior School, near Bath, thanked me for keeping e-mail contact with the school throughout the project. He went on to say that one of the boys had been so inspired by what I had done, he wanted to do a sponsored walk for the project's charity and asked that I might go along to watch.

How could I refuse to watch this young man, Russell Newman, walk 100 metres in 16 minutes and raise £120. Russell has cerebral palsy and has a one-to-one helper. He is in a wheelchair and finds it severely painful to even stand in his callipers, let alone walk. This is what I call real inspiration!

The hospital's director was very patient and forthright, and took us on a tour of the wards and facilities. KCMC is one of the flagship institutions of Tanzanian medical care but is woefully lacking in equipment and trained staff. The building itself is poorly maintained and the patient areas would certainly be closed under our health and safety laws. But the staff and doctors are hard working and dedicated, and get on with making the best of a bad job. When we left we all agreed this was not the place where you would want to be seriously ill or need advanced surgery.

The plight of the children here is particularly harrowing and Mary also had us lined up to help out at various aid projects in the local community. Whilst we had been visiting the KCMC the rest of the team had been out to the **Annexe for Blind Children** at Upendo, where they were going to build a field kitchen with material we had paid for and Josiah had trucked up to the site. All the cooking at the school was done over open, wood fires, which were very inefficient. So we had come up with a simple, low cost alternative which, with the muscle power of our Marines, would be completed in one working day.

MWERENI PRIMARY SCHOOL

Mwereni Primary School has 980 pupils — 445 boys and 535 girls. At present 17 of these are blind — 11 boys and 6 girls.

The school was started on 8th January 1943 under the supervision of a Roman Catholic Mission. In 1970 it was handed over to the government, at which time it was situated in the town centre. In 1986 it moved to its present site and in 1989 became an integrated school. The **Annexe for the Blind** was constructed by Moshi Round Table (No.13) who volunteered to build a dormitory and a classroom for six pupils.

The school enrols blind pupils from four districts: Moshi Municipal, Moshi Rural, Rombo and Hai. In order to cope with increasing numbers it was decided to use parental contributions to extend the accommodation by building a bigger dormitory. At the start of 1998 this had reached roof level.

At present, the academic performance of blind pupils is relatively poor because of a lack of such facilities as: Perkin braillers, portable typewriters, a thermoform machine, Braille kits, a resource room and transport.

Wednesday 4th February

The whole team went for a night out at Moshi's sports club tonight. Some of the lads were being groomed to play as 'ringers' in a grudge match against Arusha, scheduled for Saturday afternoon. They take their rugby **very** seriously round here and desperately want to win this fixture as they have lost on the last three meetings. And, just to try to even it out still more in Moshi's favour, I've been asked to referee!

As we had an early start the next day for our safari into the Arusha National Park, Jon, Peter, Mark, Mary and I decided to leave the sports club early. As we headed for the compound gate a deputation of teachers appeared led by Debbie Canterford. They implored us not to walk back but wait for them to drive us. We said we would be fine and that we knew the track back to Phil's well enough not to get lost in the dark. It wasn't that, they said, it just wasn't safe; none of them ever walked anywhere after dark.

Someone even offered to drive us, then and there, if we insisted on leaving, but we were adamant. There were five of us; we had our head torches; we would be fine. They were really upset when we still insisted on walking back on our own but we did feel we could look after ourselves.

So, their protestations still ringing in our ears, we set off for our camp. It was a soft night, like velvet, with a three-quarter moon and an African sky ablaze with stars. Once our eyes had adjusted to night vision we didn't need our torches. The trail was easy to follow and not even too badly rutted. The African night is full of noises much louder than the daytime. We played a game, trying to identify the sounds of individual creatures and insects. Some frogs produce a very distinctive boom and cicadas are unmistakable anywhere in the world.

We'd gone about half-a-mile when we started to notice eyes glowing in the dark out at the edge of our vision. We had all spotted shapes tracking back and forth, so we decided to turn on our torches to get a better look at the owners. We shone the powerful beams of our climbing lights and the eyes glowed redly back at us — pi dogs! These are the mangy, horrible curs which kept us awake at night with their incessant howling. There were three of them out there and, as we moved forward so they moved away, always circling out and back, keeping well away from us and not making any kind of noise. We knew that when these dogs formed packs they could be dangerous, attacking and killing anything they could drag down. But these three weren't brave and would not bother us.

However, as we neared Phil's compound, the numbers grew and often we could see six or eight dogs on the track in front of us. And now they were getting braver, standing longer and letting us approach closer before breaking away. We decided to show them who was boss in this neck of the woods and each gathered a handful of rocks. Next time they moved in we let them have it. They didn't like that. The ones we hit legged it yelping, their tails between their legs. The others soon followed. Discretion being the better part of valour, they stayed well out of range after that but followed us all the way back to the camp.

The feeling of quiet menace had been quite real and I'm glad I didn't have to face them alone. We were also told later that a local man had been hacked to death with a parang (Malaysian for machete) not far from Moshi, whilst walking back to his *shamba* alone after dark. However, I don't think any of us felt really threatened at any time while we were there and you're probably as much at risk on a Saturday night in any big city centre in the UK. You just have to be aware of a different set of risks and take appropriate precautions.

Despite the fact that they posed no real danger the damn pi dogs kept us awake on and off through all that night with their infernal yapping, yelping and howling. I don't think any of us would object to pi dog hunting!

Thursday 5th February
Next morning, after our usual breakfast of tea, toast and ration pack porridge, we met up with Hasain, our driver and guide, for the day trip to Arusha. Hasain had proved to be a good find. He was reliable and understood the European's obsession with punctuality. If asked to be somewhere at a certain time he always turned up, which is a godsend when one is trying to organise a trip requiring complicated logistics. He also speaks very good English and knows all there is to know about the region. He had brought along a second Toyota minibus and driver for the day and the team quickly split up between them.

The team had, by this time, become very *them* and *us* — *them* being the main body and *us* being the advance party. It didn't prove to be really divisive, but the split occurred because we were geographically separated and the main party felt I should have kept them more informed on the day-to-day issues. My defence is that each day they where briefed on what was required of them to fulfil the project tasks and after those were completed their time was their own. Those people who sat around waiting for me to tell them what to do next had a long wait! Anyway, the team divided quite naturally into the two vehicles and we set off for Arusha.

It was another gloriously hot, clear day and the drive up to the Park was a pleasure. We were able to relax and just take in the scenery. I felt better than I had done for quite some time; the pressure was off and I felt good.

The park was very, very beautiful. I couldn't believe the profusion of wildlife around the Ngurdoto crater and lakes — buffalo, baboon, giraffe, warthog, dik-dik, impala, hippo and water buck. What was even more amazing was the lack of people! We only saw one other tourist vehicle the whole day. It was great.

We had a lunch of chicken sandwiches, safari lager and pineapple fritters at the Momella Lodge. It was weird. There was this big game lodge with a restaurant, a bar and thatched guest lodges, all set up and ready to go, but with no guests! This beautiful place, in a fabulous location surrounded by wildlife was empty!

After lunch Hasain took us to a variety of locations around the Park and gave us a grandstand view of both Mount Kilimanjaro and Mount Meru. As we climbed up into the rain forest belt the trail was blocked by a tree which had been struck by lightning and it took all our efforts to drag it clear. It was also inundated with fire ants, which soon had the team engaged in a mad highland fling.

On our way back to Moshi we stopped at what had once been a first class hotel. And again we were faced with the Marie Celeste. The pool was empty, as was the bar, restaurant and all the guest rooms! The staff, however, seemed glad to see us. They fussed over the delivery of our cold beers, Cokes and Seven-ups, then hovered attentively, ready to fulfil our every need. It's really sad to see all this natural talent going to waste.

Later, Hasain explained to me that corruption is so bad in Tanzania that money, as he put it, 'just walks out the door'. I can well believe it. He also said that it is extremely difficult to attract foreign investment because of the *overheads*, which can turn what should be a profitable business venture into a lost cause.

So much could be done here to improve tourism and, in turn, the economy that I just can't believe the Tanzanian Government can't see the potential. For this country could be the equal of Kenya in every way! Such opportunities set my mind spinning with fantasies of running my own trekking company, or guiding service or five star hotel!

Back at Phil's reality sets in and I wonder how I would cope with living here full-time, like the Brice Bennetts up at Marangu, and Sandra, who has been teaching at the International School for twelve years. The answer is, 'I don't know.' Do you ever get used to the weather and the shortage of European food, no TV and few mod cons? Maybe the people who live here look on the lack of those as a plus!

For a man who is the head of primary education at an International School in the heart of Africa, who originates from Walsall, married a Columbian and speaks fluent, elegant Spanish with her, then I guess this is normal! But could I, or would I really want to, do it? Could I adapt, or does it take a very special kind of person to make the transition? Once again my head is filled with what might be and recollections of what might have been if I had pursued other ideas on other days. These people went out and changed their lives. Will I ever be bold enough to change mine? If you always do what you've always done you will always get what you always got!

Friday 6th February

This was to be our last, full working day before we started to wind everything up for our return to the UK on Monday. Mary, Jon, Pete, Janet, Barry, Simon and I would go to the **Mkombozi Street Kids Project**. The rest of the team would be working at the International School, taking a variety of sports' courses.

The Mkombozi project is run by Kate McAlpine — a small, bubbly, vivacious, extrovert Brit, who speaks fluent Swahili and can turn the air blue in both languages equally effectively! She and Mary hit it off straightaway and got on famously the whole time we were there.

The project is run by **Poverty Africa**. Their mission is to alleviate poverty in Africa on a sustainable basis, through implementing local community programmes to improve the living conditions of the poor by their own initiatives and effort. The kids at Mkombozi have been, and sometimes still are, living rough on the streets after having either been abandoned, orphaned or running away from home.

The thing we found most shocking was the absence of girls at the project. There are no female children at Mkombozi. Any girl child, of whatever age, left on the streets quickly disappears. They are most often abducted, raped and murdered, or kept in brothels or sold. As Kate explained:

'Street children will be the lost generation if something is not done to help them. If they are not given the skills to support themselves as adults they will become criminals purely as a means of survival. Tanzania is a country of untapped potential. Street children are a particularly poignant example of this. Abandoned, these children never learn the basic life skills needed to have any sort of happy and productive future.'

The children at Mkombozi need everyone's help. We gave them what we could. Janet, our team doctor, examined the children, while the rest of us started organising games and lessons to show the children how to use the things we had brought for them — bats and balls, paper, paints and coloured crayons. Assuming that they knew what Christmas was, for them this was it!

Janet was appalled by the diseases: bilharzia from drinking infected water, ringworm, dysentery, gonorrhoea and eczema, to mention but a few. There was no supply of tap water, so all the water used for drinking, cooking and cleaning came from a nearby stream. And the sanitation, such as it was, was hard to describe.

This is no reflection on Kate and the other workers on the Project. You cannot conjure from thin air the things which you need to remedy such crises. Most times the children only had *ugali* and beans to eat, cooked on an open wood fire. As at most schools the children stood up to eat.

The building had only three, bare rooms, with two fold-away tables and no chairs. At night thin, stained mattresses are laid on the concrete floor with blankets spread over them. This is where the children will spend the night — uncomfortable but, hopefully, safe.

Many of the children at Mkombozi have special educational and emotional needs. Some have never attended school before. Many have behavioural disorders. These range from attention deficit disorder and mental retardation to alcohol and drug abuse. Many have been physically, sexually and emotionally abused.

I, and the others, wished that we could have stayed longer and done more to help. We all found this place particularly distressing. For anyone who would like to help or contribute to the Mkombozi Street Kids Project, Kate's contact address at **Poverty Africa** can be found at the back.

Without a Social Services' safety net or a National Health Service, in a country with an economy in crisis, there is a desperate shortage of nearly everything needed to build a sustainable infrastructure. Teachers, doctors and nurses often don't get paid for weeks or months. Equipment is often old, badly maintained or non-existent. How they get so far on so little is nothing short of amazing. These people could flourish on what we discard as obsolete.

I think some of the Aid agencies are missing the point here! Instead of donating money they should be getting people to donate old Perkin braille machines, typewriters, books, paper and pencils, out-of-date medicine. ('Out-of-date is better than none at all', I was told.) Wake up out there! Enough, it's easy to get carried away.

Saturday 7th February

Today we started packing up the gear we would be bringing back to the UK and sorting out what could be left behind. The whole team met up at the school ready for the big game in the afternoon. Having been fitted out in borrowed boots and shorts, we all set off for the Moshi Club, where the game would be played. This must be the most spectacular rugby pitch in the entire world, not to mention the view from the clubhouse! The pitch itself is nothing to write home about; it angles gently upwards and the grass is hummocky and sparse. But with Kilimanjaro as the backdrop, dominating the whole horizon between the far posts, it is, without doubt, the most dramatic sporting arena.

As the afternoon wore on tension began to mount with the expected arrival of the Arusha team. Then, at the eleventh hour, a telephone message came through to the Club to say that Arusha were cancelling because they couldn't raise a team! This was greeted with howls of delight and derision from the Moshi players and fans, who claimed it as a victory! One can only assume the opposition had heard that we were playing!

It was decided that we shouldn't let a good afternoon's sport go to waste, so we split the team in two and had a game of seven-a-side instead. I was struggling to keep up and I was only the ref! The temperature must have been in the high nineties and it was humid. With the sun blazing down out of a clear, tropical sky, the lads just poured with sweat. But it proved to be a very entertaining game, played with real spirit.

Today was also Janet's 29th birthday and we surprised her with a specially commissioned cake!

The end was in sight and so we celebrated for our various reasons. We would all take away something different from the Project. We had become a team; we had done our best and that for me, is good enough.

Sunday 8th February
Today, our last day in Tanzania, Phil and friends had decided to send us off in style with a huge barbecue. Last minute packing was done and transport to the airport organised. We haven't been here long but we feel as if we've known each other forever. By four o'clock the *barbie* was cooking and a whole load of people had arrived for our farewell bash, all bearing food and booze! Rob Jones and his French wife, Martine, arrived with a haunch of Thompson's gazelle, which went whole onto the fire. It was a real colonial-style party and we had a great time, exchanging gifts, addresses and telephone numbers, and issuing invitations to visit.

The gazelle was cooked and distributed amongst the carnivores. Mary took one bite, gagged and disappeared to the toilet! Funny, mine tasted OK and everyone else seemed to be enjoying theirs too! When she returned to the fray she told us, 'It wasn't the taste, it was the thought of eating Bambi.' Africa is not a place for the sensitive.

During the morning we had visited the market place in Moshi to collect our contributions for the party and it had all the colour and vibrancy that one expects in an African market. The diversity of goods on offer is phenomenal, as are the smells, not just from the piles of spices, vegetables and fruit, but also from the not too freshly butchered meat, hung or laid out covered in flies and sweating in the heat. I'm glad we hadn't seen it before we'd been out eating steaks!

However, these guys sure know how to party and the barbecue went on far into the night. Most of the team couldn't stand the pace and, knowing that we had a long flight next day, we made our excuses and headed for the tents.

Monday 9th February

This morning Phil's house and garden looked like the aftermath of a rock festival! We had arranged to rendezvous at the school car park and Hasain was there waiting for us, as punctual as ever. It was a subdued scene as we packed our gear aboard for the last time. Many of our friends from the school had come to see us off and there was genuine emotion in that last farewell. The trip to the airport was uneventful and our last shillings were spent on souvenirs before we boarded the plane. As the 747 unwound off the tarmac I couldn't help feeling sad. It was all over. We were going home.

From Jon:
It was time to leave the many friends we had made here in Tanzania over the past three, chaotic weeks. Before then we were total strangers, yet they had offered us the help and hospitality normally associated with long-standing friendship.

So many thoughts kept passing through my mind. I was delighted to be returning home to my family but there was much to complete on the fund-raising side of the project, as well as catching up with my own work. And I could not help but ponder that, even though we had done so much in so short a time, for me the main task had not been accomplished.

The journey to the airport was rather solemn. The snow-capped summit of Kilimanjaro glistened in the sunshine, drawing both my eyes and thoughts like a magnet. One day I would be back ...

From Janet Hastle, the Expedition's Doctor ...

I was excited at the prospect of joining an expedition to climb Mount Kilimanjaro, although I applied for the position with great trepidation. Working as an RAF doctor in the Falklands at the time I was anxious about how I was going to contribute to the preparations from such a distance. I also wondered if my experience working in a rehabilitation unit for disabled servicemen and women would be sufficient to assist Jon in his endeavour. As a female would I be fit enough and strong enough too, or would I be seen as a burden in this record breaking attempt? However, I was smitten by the idea and had to give it a go.

I applied and waited. Shortly after I returned to the UK, in the depths of Winter and on a soggy, cold Saturday, I made my way to meet the team at Blencathra in the Lake District, which was to be the testing ground for both team and wheelchair. There seemed to be an awful lot of people there and a lot of preparation still to be completed. The day was a success however and, despite the weather and the over-enthusiastic attempts to attach the tow lines to the chair, lift, push, pull and propel it, we arrived at the top and, perhaps more importantly, got back down to the bottom of the mountain all in one piece. We also realised that both the chair and our organisation in assisting Jon needed more than a few modifications!

I was impressed and compelled to continue, mostly due to my impression of Jon. At this point the team was a mix of experience and expertise, enthusiasm and uncertainty. Jon, on the other hand, was so impressive, approachable, organised and charismatic, which alone was enough to convince anyone that this project would work. For the venture to achieve its goals, to attract sponsorship for the British Wheelchair Sports Foundation and to promote the awareness of disability in sport, Jon needed some help through us and I now felt I fitted the bill.

Individual efforts continued apace but I didn't feel like a team member. I gathered together my medical kit and advised on immunisations and, more importantly, attempted to obtain publicity and sponsorship. The latter I found an embarrassing, alien, difficult task, asking people for money, talking on the radio and writing pieces for newspapers and magazines.

Eventually the day arrived to set off and I made my way to the airport and waited an infinity for everyone to turn up. Conrad had managed an impressive feat, transporting 40 weighty boxes of ration packs across London. Before the others joined us we attempted to negotiate their speedy and free transfer onto the Alliance air transport — the first major snag, but a good way to gel with your fellow travellers. The expedition proper began. The flight was unexpectedly comfortable and reassuringly beneficial. Further snags and bribes didn't surface until the customs' farce in Tanzania!

The rest is history and described elsewhere. From the medical viewpoint there's not much to tell. Jon, of course, stoical as ever, was the least of my worries. Due to his foresight and preparation he did not succumb to the effects of cold, pressure sores, cramp, injury or dehydration. Heseemed also to be less affected by altitude than most, and my only concern was his eating and sleeping. These both suffered because of his perfectionism and continual concern and involvement in all aspects of the expedition, from its promotion and public relations, to its grass roots organisation and the keeping up of team morale.

Others suffered more profoundly from the effects of altitude. This was little more than I had expected, considering the unprecedented amount of effort the climb eventually required and the rapidity with which we ascended due to the route and bureaucracy. All went well though, with some descending and others resting at appropriate times. And I did feel that my opinion was both welcomed and acted upon on these occasions.

As far as the expedition went, I feel privileged to have been a part of a supreme achievement. Jon soared in my estimation. As time wore on everybody's role emerged and we began to work together. Some people felt better able to contribute to the donkey work but everybody did their stint without being pressurised. Everyone also fulfilled their primary role with enthusiasm and commitment.

Despite the difficulties, we never lost sight of the goal and sensible decisions were made after due discussion with all involved. There were, inevitably, frictions in the team but all were minor and mainly directed towards the BBC's cameraman!

I was proud of myself also as, with all such expeditions, one inevitably learns many valuable lessons. I was impressed by my own stamina and the contribution I made to the team as a whole, quite apart from my medical skills, which fortunately were not required very much. Most of all I was impressed by Jon, who is more able than most able bodied but none-the-less faced difficulties about which I had not thought, such as the feeling of helplessness and imprisonment when we arrived at the hut each night. It was difficult for him to venture from his bunk as we merrily pottered around doing our domestic chores.

I learnt also about pride and stubbornness, that there is a way of asking for help and a way of assisting, which all of us need from time to time. This incurs no loss of pride and still permits determination and self reliance in all other aspects of life. I feel this is a key to coming to terms with life in general and disability in particular.

During the final week when we visited hospitals, orphanages and schools, I have to admit that I felt somewhat uncomfortable with the whole experience, though I appreciate that we did contribute. As a health professional I felt I had a lot to offer but it was difficult to understand the different priorities and politics in a week in order to do something really meaningful. It's one thing to diagnose a problem, whether it be clinical or material, but quite another to do something about it. I felt shocked at the unnecessary suffering experienced by the children and the infirm, in a country rich in natural resources.

After returning to the UK I had to face the flack about being on the BBC news with hair not washed for a week. And I still had the most difficult task to perform, collecting the sponsorship money and writing yet more newspaper articles. Just give me a mountain anyday!

Janet Hastle

From Mary Groves, Base Camp Manager ...

I was invited to go to Kilimanjaro as Base Camp Manager with an expedition group assisting a disabled athlete, Jon Amos, to get as far up the mountain as possible.

My part was to stay at base camp, to organise transport and deliver sports gear to under-privileged schools. These schools did not have games on their school timetable because they did not have any basic PE equipment — not even a football. So my gifts were very much appreciated.

Another of my tasks was to find out how we could help various projects whilst we were there with either equipment or manpower, for example, teaching, giving talks and, at one stage, building a field kitchen for an annexe for blind children. The kitchen they had was disgusting; when it rained rivers of water simply put the fire out. We also did community work in and around Moshi.

I had spoken with Moshi's International School before going out to Africa and discussed my work in child care with the life skills' teacher, Debbie Canterford. I had asked her if she knew of any residential child care project with which I could get involved during my stay, so that the information I gathered could be shared with my colleagues and the children at the college where I worked in England.

Newland Group Child Care, based in Hull, had agreed to my joining the expedition for nearly a month if I could achieve this. Debbie said she would arrange for me to meet Kate McAlpine, the project co-ordinator for the Mkombozi Centre for Street Children as soon as I arrived in Moshi. I was really thrilled with this and looked forward to my visit.

At our first meeting Kate said how delighted she was to meet someone with my experience in child care and invited me to the Centre the following day. I really did not know what to expect as I was already appalled by the poverty around me.

We were taken by land rover as the roads out there were dreadful. Jon came too as he had been in care as a young child and wanted to see what childcare was like in Africa. The wheels squelched through the muddy tracks to Mkombozi and the building looked quite derelict. Then about twenty boys ran out, shouting and smiling. They held onto our hands and tried to help Jon with his wheelchair — all grinning and chattering. Kate then came over to greet us and show us round the Centre.

Outside, there was a compound which served as a play area, a classroom, where children sat on logs to hear stories, and a cooking area. Inside, there were two large rooms, each having a large table. The children had to stand up to eat their meals at these tables, or to have their lessons if it was raining outside, as there were no chairs. During my stay I taught crafts and other activities in that room.

As there were no washing facilities the children had to wash in the filthy river, which meant that many of them had severe sores, worms and various parasitic infections which can only be found in Africa. Lunch was cooked outside over a wood fire. A massive cauldron bubbled away full of maize and red beans — the staple diet of poor people wherever we went. To me it just looked like wallpaper paste and I never did pluck up enough courage to try it.

At night the tables were taken outside and very thin, dirty mattresses were laid on the bare floor before equally dirty, woollen blankets were given out, as Tanzania gets really cold at night. All the children slept in a heap together and Kate did say there had been cases where older boys had raped younger ones. Also of great concern to me was the fact that only one male member of staff slept with the boys at night. He was only paid the equivalent of £30 a month and had no childcare qualifications at all.

I spoke at length with Kate about my fears as I felt that if she was trying to stop them selling their bodies in town, only to be sexually abused at Mkombozi, they would maybe leave, feeling that at least they were getting paid for this in town. She agreed with the points I was making but they just did not have any money for more workers.

Mary Groves

From Conrad Trickett, Logistics Support Group ...

In addition to the Marines on this trip there was a bizarre cluster of civilians, including prison officers, ex-military and, to enhance the overall appeal, a female RAF doctor! We came together to assist Jon Amos to power himself to the summit of Kilimanjaro, at 19,340 feet the highest mountain in Africa. Looking at Jon's Great Britain weight lifting champion's frame though, we wouldn't need to do much assisting.

On Arrival

The nine hour flight to Tanzania passed pleasantly enough, assisted by the effective sleeping drug of Kronenburg and red wine. We then awoke to find the reality of dealing with local bureaucracy. The advance party informed us that, despite prior arrangements, we were now no longer allowed to camp on the hill or spend eight days on the climb. The National Park was only going to allow us five days and charge us double for the pleasure! To top it all, the rear axle broke on the Toyota taking us to our base camp. Things could only get better!

Climbing Kilimanjaro

Day One: It was raining heavily as we set off from Marangu Gate at about 6,000 feet, the track cutting through rain forest to the Mandara Hut — about 9,000 feet. On the way we discovered that tree roots and wheelchairs don't mix too well. Add a bit of mud and the fun really begins. Robbie reminisced about mud runs and endurance courses, while we lifted, pushed, pulled, slipped and slid our way up to the hut.

Day Two: It's strange how epic days start so nonchalantly. The weather was drier, the path wider and the tree roots smaller. Four or five hours of pushing and pulling later our guide (loose definition) informed us we had half to go. 'Half-an-hour?' we quizzed. 'No, halfway to the hut.' Gob-smacked was redefined!

The next seven or eight hours are legendary. Imagine a rocky path too rocky for a wheelchair to bounce over or swerve around. Imagine this path cutting through a steep-sided re-entrant. Imagine seven such re-entrants. Throw in a couple of hours of darkness, plus eleven stones of wheelchair and occupant, and you have the makings of a legend! More than twelve hours after leaving Mandara the lights of the Horombo hut appeared at about 12,000 feet. The team was drained. If tomorrow followed a similar pattern we were in trouble. Morale wavered briefly but a big meal and plenty of banter brought us back to our usual selves.

Day Three: The vegetation zone of yesterday gave way to alpine desert, and a track capable of taking a land rover stretched in front of us. We stormed onward and upward into the thinner air. The BBC man vomited and turned back; a team member vomited and carried on. The trekkers cheered as we pulled into the Kibo hut (about 15,500 feet) only 20 minutes behind normal guidebook time.

About this time our team photographer started to behave even more bizarrely than usual, wandering around looking for snow when the snow line was 250m (feet) above us! The altitude was beginning to show.

Day Four: We set off shortly after midnight to ascend the scree and snow leading to the crater rim which, although frozen, was easier to ascend. The team was already reduced in numbers by several suffering with the altitude too badly to continue safely. A slow pace moved us up towards our goal. However, at about 16,500 feet we reached the snow line and had a team chat. With a reduced and exhausted team, dubious conditions ahead and concerns over the descent, we made the decision to turn around.

Back at the Kibo hut we grabbed a few hours sleep before continuing the descent to Horombo. As with the ascent the track here was excellent for the wheelchair and Jon would often leave us standing as he shot off into the distance. We all felt better in the thicker air back at Horombo and, although disappointed at our lack of summit success, we knew we had given everything in the attempt.

Day Five: There was almost a punch-up (in Marine language) when we learnt of a so-called land rover trail which winds its way up to Horombo. 'Why hadn't we ascended on it?' Evidently it is only used as an emergency route to get vehicles high up on the mountain, but trekkers can descend on it. As we cruised down to an altitude lower than our starting point we all considered the 'What ifs?' What if we had known of this route a week earlier **and** had negotiated to ascend it? But it was a big AND.

We soon reached a track and dispatched our guide to find some transport to take us back to base camp. In the meantime a bar (shack!) was discovered and a couple of bottles of the local brew downed. Time moved on and, with still no sign of our guide, we set off on foot, the village children dancing after Jon in his wheelchair. Then, out of nowhere, a 29-seater bus appeared on the dirt track with the smiling face of our guide in the passenger seat. The journey was over, base camp and bed lay ahead.

Afterwards

After a good night's sleep and essential administration we set about a full programme of teaching sports to the local school and assisting in various community projects in and around Moshi. Swimming, volleyball, football, gymnastics and life saving were all coached.

We built a wood burning stove at the local blind school and beat the local rugby team at seven-a-side. Inevitably, a couple of social functions were also programmed in, as was a tour of a local safari park.

Achievements

Team spirit throughout the trip was excellent. Jon achieved a new world altitude record on the mountain and we are all still involved with fund raising for *The British Wheelchair Sports Foundation*. A famous mountaineering quote on expedition priorities says, 'Come back, come back friends, climb the mountain.' I suppose two out of three ain't bad!

Conrad Trickett

EPILOGUE

After our return to the UK the team went its separate ways. Mark, Barney and I returned to our jobs as Physical Education officers. Conrad resigned his commission in the Royal Marines and joined the Grampian police force. (His wife shortly afterwards gave birth to their first child.) Simon and Robbie are still in the Royal Marines, Robbie recently having been promoted to Sergeant. Janet is still doctoring in the RAF; Pete and Barry lecture in Information Technology and Photography respectively. Mary is currently setting up her own outreach project to work with disadvantaged children and Nick is still studying to become an engineer.

Jon has returned to his normal, hectic life of coaching, lecturing and training. In recognition of the team's efforts we were voted *Team of the Year* for 1998 by *The British Wheelchair Sports Foundation* which, for Jon, can be added to his *Coach of the Year* award for 1997.

Jon and I are currently planning for his next venture, the *Man-of-Steel Trans-Australia Challenge*, due to take place in July and August 1999. In this Jon will attempt to cross Australia from north to south, Darwin to Adelaide, by handcycle — a distance of over 2,000 miles — to set a new world record and raise money to fund the development of education and training programmes for the *Wheelchair Sports Worldwide Foundation*.

The crossing has been attempted several times but no-one has yet succeeded. Jon intends to change that! Robbie and Simon will once again form the core of Jon's support team. We also hope to carry out some useful research work during the crossing, into the effects of high intensity endurance exercise in the heat on the paraplegic athlete.

The whole African experience was a great success and, although we failed to summit, we succeeded in setting a new record which, hopefully, will inspire others to follow in Jon's tracks. It has been an enormous personal triumph for Jon and a period of outstanding achievement for us all, which we hope will continue.

We made many friends, had a little adventure and, in the process, discovered some more about ourselves, our world and our place in it.

Derek Groves

A FINAL WORD FROM JON AMOS

We would like to thank all our sponsors, both material and financial, large or small, for their part in the success of this project and for their faith in us. A special mention must go to Dave Lynch and *Visual Eyes* for enabling us to share the project with thousands around the world through the Bluedome web site and to its readers who sent goodwill messages.

All the values, aims and objectives which Derek Groves and I included in our promotional booklet have been carried out, which in itself is an achievement. Not only did we create a 'world first' by getting someone higher on a mountain in a wheelchair than anyone has been before, some 16,040 feet, but we also achieved the following:

1) **Awareness of what people with disabilities can achieve when they concentrate on their abilities rather than their disabilities.** This was achieved through the worldwide BBC television news service and coverage on national news programmes throughout the day. We also gave live radio interviews and appeared on BBC One and Two, Channels Four and Five, and various regional programmes. Press articles appeared in The Times, the Daily Telegraph, the People, Daily Mirror and various local papers. The full-time coverage given on the Bluedome Internet Site further endorsed our world-wide media coverage. Our video of the trip has already been accepted for an international symposium to be held in Spain in May 1999 and there's also this book — which you are now reading!

2) **Through cultural exchange within the host country** we supplied our coaching and educational expertise and gave both educational and sporting equipment to areas of grea need. We have also now 'adopted' three projects which we hope to help with further resources. These are:

   The Street Kids Project in Mkombozi

   The Annexe for Blind Children at Mwereni Primary School

   The KCMC Hospital

The needs of all three are basic. They could make good use of many materials which, with our advanced technology, we might discard. We would like to ask anyone who might feel able to offer resources such as wheelchairs, Braille typewriters or basic educational materials, to contact us using the information given below, or through our e-mail address, which is: roof_of_africa_on_wheels@cableinet.co.uk

Jon Amos
Sunnynook, 19 Stanway, Bitton, Bristol, BS30 6JU.
Fax/Tel: 0117 949 3536

Derek Groves
26 North Promenade, Withernsea, East Yorkshire, HU19 2DW.
Fax/Tel: 01964 615603

Information is also on our Internet website:

www.bluedome.co.uk/jonamos/jonamosnewindex.htm

Addresses in Tanzania

Mkombozi Centre for Street Children
PO Box 9601
Kilimanjaro road Post Office
Moshi
Tanzania

Poverty Africa (main office)
PO Box 8622
Dar es Salaam
Tanzania

Josia Mchome, CAS scheme co-ordinator
PO Box 733
Moshi
Tanzania
E-mail: ISMOSHI@maf.org

ACKNOWLEDGMENTS

Shaun Davis and Ray Penhaligon, of New Station Road Bodyworks, Bristol — for supplying promotional vehicle and advertising space for additional sponsors.

Stuart Dunne and *Cyclone Wheelchairs*, Ellesmere Port, for supplying wheelchair, tracker and technical support.

Wheelchair Spares and Technical Support from:
    Kieron Slocombe of Wheeltech
    Vinny Ross of Chevron

Dave Lynch of *Bluedome*, for supplying and maintaining web pages.

Promotional Material supplied by:
    Alan Ayres and Glen May of Robert Home Paper Co. Ltd.
    Chris and Tim Bates — graphic design
    Earl and Ludlow — printers
    Vinyl Graphics of Bristol

Royal Marines — for food and logistical support

Royal Air Force — for medical support.

Neil McAdie of *North Cape* — principal clothing sponsor

Danielle Gaillard-Picher of *Camelbak* — for hydration systems.

Telecommunication Systems and Technical Support from
    David Watkins of *Carphone Warehouse*
    Chris Wood of *Applied Satellite Technology*

Media Coverage Worldwide — BBC TV and Radio

Our thanks also go to the following (in no particular order) for supporting *Roof of Africa on Wheels,* **either financially or materially:**

Ricoh
Cableinet/Telewest
Brasher Boot Company
Alliance Air
Dave Bates/Alfred Bekker
Royal and Sun Alliance
Miles Better Foods
Fuji
Seton Healthcare
Berghaus
Troll
Man o'Leisure
Timberland
BAE - Brough
BT - Bristol PR and Communications
Dan Harfords Motors, Bristol
Geoff Treasure's Cleaning Services
Wet and Wild
Fotostop - Bristol
Fotoprocessing of Hull
Staff at HM Prison, Hull
Staff and Inmates at HM Prison, Eastwood Park
Princes Quay, Hull
Russell Newman
John Woods Cycles, Bristol
Motability Finance
Octavius Hunt
Local and National Press
Stuart Moull Chemists, Bristol

... and to all other wellwishers, whether individuals, schools or groups, who sponsored *Roof of Africa on Wheels.*